121 Strategies for Bully Proofing Your School!

Insights, Tips, Stories, Activities, AND Reproducible Worksheets
>> Grades 6-10

by Erika Karres, Ed.D.
Author of the bestselling book
Mean Chicks, Cliques and Dirty Tricks

youthlight inc. TRANSFERRED TO YRDSB

© 2009 by YouthLight, Inc.
Chapin, SC 29036

Cover Design by Graphic Solutions
Book Design and Layout by Diane Florence
Project Editing by Susan Bowman

ISBN: 978-1-59850-066-0

Library of Congress Number
2008943806

10 9 8 7 6 5 4 3 2 1
Printed in the United States

121 Strategies for
Bully Proofing
Your School

For teachers, principals, guidance counselors, resource officers, parents, grandparents, school nurses, PTA/PTO members, school board members, student services directors, faith group members, medical technicians, hospital staffers, government workers, recreation assistants, youth advocates, juvenile probation and parole officers, community volunteers, child issues researchers, policy developers, psychologists, family therapists, media representatives, and all bully survivors.

Contents

Contents

Dedication

This book is dedicated to **you**, the special person who just picked up this book. I know why. It's because you **care**, because you want to make a difference, and because you can.

Yes, **you** can make a big difference in preventing bullying and unnecessary pain and violence. And you will, once you realize just how much your caring, input, and actions are needed to deal with this problem. On behalf of all kids in America and around the world, I would like to express my heart-felt gratitude to you because you have it in your power to prevent bullying and violence, and to change lives and maybe even save some of them.

Some day when you look back on your work, you will feel good about what you took from this book to make use of, because it helped. You decreased the level of bullying and violence around you. **You** made a big difference. Thank you again.

Acknowledgments

A special thank-you to
- Dr. Bob and Susan Bowman for their excellent work and deep commitment to improving the lives of all our young people, and thereby the state of our nation, now and in the future. Since our nation sets the example for the rest of the world, the Bowmans' powerful, positive, and peaceful influence can be felt all around the globe.

- My two brilliant, beautiful, and giving daughters, Elizabeth Shearin Hounshell, RN, and Mary Denise Shearin, MD, and my devoted husband, Andrew Matthew Karres, for their steadfast support and unwavering love.

How to Use This Book

This book is *your* anti-bully help-book and resource guide. It explains how you can take a stand against bullying and youth violence. As such, it needs your involvement, input, and hands-on approach. Just like a pair of walking shoes in the closet does no good (unless you're swatting a brown recluse spider with them), so does this book no good if you don't really use it. Scribble all over it. Fold some pages or tear them out, to reproduce and use. Post the red flags of bullying and violence proneness or cut out a sentence and "magnet" it to your fridge.

Pass this book around. Leave it in the work lounge. Keep it in the glove compartment to read while waiting for traffic to un-jam, okay? Most importantly, please use this book with your students—in a lesson, as a source of worksheets, for homework assignments, or as a discussion starter. In short, use this book up.

This book contains much more than 121 strategies, stories, tips, lessons plans, and hand-outs straight from the files of the experts—professionals who bully proof their schools and communities year after year. Put some or all of these strategies and worksheets to use at the start of a new term, camp experience, sports season, or later in the year. They are very adaptable to your circumstances and grade level. Small groups can also be bully proofed, and individual bullies can be worked with. In fact, all kids, no matter in what setting, can benefit enormously from these bully and violence prevention strategies.

Why This Book Now?

Of all the huge social ills we face today, the sharp rise in the bullying and aggressive behavior of our kids can be called the most devastating one because it is so widespread and has so many tragic consequences. Bullying and youth violence don't just diminish or debilitate our society. They can flat-out kill you. And your kids, your other relatives, your friends, plus all our hopes for a bright and shiny future.

No nation can flourish while its heart—in the form of its youngest members, our kids—is under vicious attack by the terminal illness of unchecked bully behavior. And while some inroads have recently been made and some anti-bully programs have been instituted here and there, this effort has been scant and piece-meal, and the results have been similar—scant and piece-meal, instead of being spot-on and peace-filled.

Therefore, we need to reverse this vicious trend. We can't wait until more acts of aggressive behavior by our kids occur. We need to catch this deadly disease early—at the pre-bully and pre-violent stage. For this reason, this quick, compelling paperback is on an important mission: To inform you about the main types of bullies, about the warning signs of bullying and youth violence, and about what you can do to stop it. Many of the solutions are those used by professionals who have given their whole lives to working with bullies. Therefore, this book is a crucial and empowering must-read for all teachers, principals, school advisors, counselors, social workers, coaches, law enforcement professionals, parents, grandparents, church-, temple-, and mosque leaders, bully survivors, and community members in general—in fact, for anyone who cares about protecting our youth from the scourge of bullies and violence.

We all need to know how to bully proof our schools. And now we can.
Let's get started. Time is of the essence.

Word of Caution

The terms "pre-bullying" and "pre-violence" are used like the terms "pre-diabetes" or "pre-cancer." They mean conditions are conducive to leading to much more serious problems. In health, that means that a diagnosis of a pre-illness indicates a need for major life-style change. In children, a label of pre-bullying or pre-violence also means a change is needed, for tragically, pre-bullying and pre-violence can set the stage for deadly bullying and violence later.

But even with our best intentions, it's not easy to completely bully proof a kid or school. What causes a climate conducive to bullying can also be complicated. Too bad we can't bubble-wrap all children, tuck them away, and declare them 100% bully proofed forever. Even if we could keep them away from outside bully influences and rid them of all inner aggressive urges, there is always the chance that a new development has been overlooked. Therefore, the terms "bully proof" and "violence proof" are not like the term "water proof." Water proofed material will keep water out.

But we're dealing with human beings—kids who are living, breathing, and in the process of becoming—not things. So just like the phrase "baby-proofing a room" can't guarantee 100% that a super smart baby somewhere won't find a way to get in trouble, so can we not guarantee that using the 121 bully proofing strategies will be a magic formula.

But count on this: Each anti-bullying strategy will go a long way toward making life better for all your students and teachers, counselors, parents, coaches, and others. And you.

Section 1: Introduction

Isn't it great to know that we can now reduce the bully behavior and violence potential in our schools? Some experts say that using the following anti-bullying strategies can reduce youth aggression by 85%. Others claim an even higher rate of reduction. Whatever the case, rest assured that you are on the forefront of stemming youth bullying.

Before we start, are you wondering why I'm so committed to this work?

My Mission

From the moment I was born, the word VICTIM was stamped across my forehead. It wasn't visible back then and isn't visible now. So why, after happily teaching public school and on the college level for 35 years, did I start going on a new mission to take on the bullies, fight violence, and stand up for victims?

I really had no choice: The circumstances of my early life forced me to it. You see, sometimes countries are the worst and most horrible bullies of them all.

My story is simple. I was born in the heart of the beast of unspeakable violence. And it has dogged me ever since. When you know something from the inside out because with your first breath you inhale its essence, isn't it your duty to go to war against it?

Let me explain. I was born at the worst time and in the worst place during the last century—at the beginning of WWII and in the midst of a horrendous war zone—the Eastern Front. As far back as I can remember, I breathed air saturated with bomb debris, fireball residue, and the smell of burned flesh. One of the first sounds I remember hearing was the staccato of wide-spread gun fire. The first faces I remember seeing were grief-stricken and tear-streaked. I didn't know what a smile was. Everyone around me was heartbroken. In the hospital where I was born, the babies' cries were drowned out by the screams of the mothers and nurses. Their husbands, brothers, fathers, and sons had been drafted into WWII and been injured or killed, or would soon be.

Worse, much worse: The Beast of Violence of WWII wasn't satisfied with just open warfare on the front. Oh no. Night and day, starting years before the onset of the actual battles, it destroyed the civilians. Completely innocent people became the worst victims: all Jews, all people who didn't go along with the Nazi regime, and anyone who complained, or was openly religious, or just different. The concentration camps devoured them all.

Life back then was like tiptoeing on an unraveling tightrope—for the lucky ones. For the damned, there was no rope, no matter how desperately they tried to live just one more day. The brutal henchmen came at all hours. That's the horrible reality I was born into—the abyss of the most horrendous violence man has ever known. It is estimated that over 50 million people lost their lives in the death camps, the bomb attacks, on the front, in the Siberian winters, and due to starvation, in less than a decade. I lost my twin brother, my older sister's twin, and my baby sister. I felt like I was born in a morgue, being surrounded by three dead babies, at least their spirits. No wonder, my mother could never look at me without pain and mourning in her eyes.

Even that stopped when my mother became a victim too. She died when I was six and I spent hours and hours by her deathbed, screaming, "Mama! Mama! Get up, get up!"

To no avail. From then on my life became even more of a nightmare. Even before that time, there was never any food, nor heat, nor water at my house. There was nothing, only whispering that told horrible tales of our neighbors being whisked away at midnight and never seen again, or of the store keeper and his family being clubbed near to death and dragged off at noon. Or of what horror befell the city of my birth **(see Conclusion)**.

As a result from birth on, I hated bullies and violence with a passion. I could never accept the awful injustice of violence as a child, nor did I during my long teaching career in North Carolina, during which I collected student notes and anecdotes—until 1999. The Columbine School tragedy was the biggest school killing at that time and took 15 lives, including those of the two teenage gunmen.

In my grief over this senseless slaughter, I wrote a poem and sent it to the affected community in Colorado. My poem was based on John Donne's poetic lament, written 400 years ago:

<u>Death, Be Not Proud</u>

> Though you have snatched much life about to flower
> Cut it all down before it reached its power
> Though you have wounded, maimed oh countless others
> Ruined the lives of moms, dads, sisters, brothers
> Though you have ripped a calm community apart
> Have pierced and injured our nation's heart
> Death, be not proud
>
> Instead, pack up. Dress in your own dark shroud
> For you have lost. No more your gruesome game
> Call off your bloody demons, scram in shame

You didn't truly make our loved ones gone
You only made them leap ahead and on and on
And now they lead us, cheer us on the way
As we take up the fight begun that very day
When they faced death and made it slink away

Now our Colorado victims stand and lead
And pull for us as everywhere they plant a seed
That grows and grows, watered by our tears
Soon, soon it blooms—to banish all our fears
Yes, it will spread and spread and help us fight
For those just gone ahead will finally unite
Us, wake us, make us strong until as one
We'll put violence and guns forever on the run

Death, be not proud. It's you that died
Who you cut down is now our shining guide

One of the many people in the Columbine school community who thanked me for the poem was Pastor David Blue Jacket, of St. Mary's Catholic Church in Littleton, Colorado. He wrote:

Thank you for the poem to use with the Columbine families.
I will also include it at the memorial in Clement Park. Please continue to pray for us.

Indeed, many of us prayed for that stricken community, and did the same for the community of Virginia Tech, where only a few years later, a student took 33 lives. The memorial service for the needlessly slaughtered kids and adults by a young purveyor of mass violence was seen on TV around the country. It spurred many people into penning more condolence letters. But what good is that afterwards?

So I knew I had to do more—nationally and internationally. I started writing books about youth violence and relational aggression because it was clear: If we stop the bullying, we can reduce the violence potential of our young, and make the world safer and freer of pain.

This book is coming out at the 10th anniversary of the Columbine shooting.

Section 2: Four Types of Bullies

This is the time when bullying ends. While the problem can be complex and metastasize if not dealt with, the solutions are here. We just have to use them. The most important reason that keeps us from using the solutions is a lack of knowledge. Too often we just don't realize who the bullies are, what they do, and how harmful their actions really are.

Sure, the most obvious members of the "vulture culture," a detrimental atmosphere that exists in many schools, are easily identified. They beat up little kids, attract attention, and are told to stop. But what about the more subtle bullies, those that hide in plain sight?

Sad to say, too often bullying goes on right before our eyes. Yet we do nothing, but not because we don't care. It's because we don't know the various bully types that can range from minor, less serious forms to major and extremely dangerous ones. But far too often, if we don't stop the lesser bullies in their tracks, they will progress and eventually do deadly harm. So being able to recognize the four kinds of bullies, and how to stop them, is key.

**Bully Type 1
The Disser**

**Bully Type 2
The Hitter**

**Bully Type 3
The Controller**

**Bully Type 4
The Potential Killer**

© YouthLight Inc.

Bully Type 1 – The Disser

Insight

The disser is a student who verbally disrespects another on purpose and belongs to the most common of the lesser bully varieties. On the surface he/she does little harm. Nobody is physically hurt and no vandalism is observable. No school rule is blatantly broken and the end result is often just a minute ripple effect. Certainly some kids got their feelings hurt, but so what? No outward signs remain.

Therefore, the dissers are the most overlooked school bullies because they shoot from the lip only. No fists or weapons are in play. And after their hurtful words have been flung and have stung, who keeps a record? Sticks and stones may hurt, but not words, is too often the unwritten rule in school. So word attacks, even of the most painful kind, are ignored.

And yet the dissers can do serious harm and leave lasting inner scars. But that doesn't enter their minds. They are really dismissers, students who think too much of themselves and too little of others. Therefore, they belong to the school "vultures," students who are bigger, older, or meaner, and verbally prey on the younger, smaller, sweeter, or less glib kids. In short, the dissers are sneaky bullies who channel their relational aggression into name-calling, threatening, hate speech, taunting, mean teasing, or socially excluding others.

Like all bullies, the dissers want to elevate their standing by belittling other kids. Their weapons of choice are their wagging tongues or their nimble fingers on a keyboard. They use language either to diss a classmate with oral communication or via techno teasing or blasting.

This is the Text Generation. That means kids love to text, using their own abbreviated language. Therefore, many disser bullies show their disrespect toward their peers in their emailing, blogging, chatting in chat rooms, texting, instant messaging, website posting, or taking pictures and forwarding them.

This verbal or written bullying is so widespread that we can subdivide it. Homophobic bullying and harassment belong to one of the subgroups. In fact, gay kids can come in for the most frequent bullying. Some researchers say that many kids hear anti-gay comments more than 25 times a day. Worse is that one third of homosexual students have been threatened and physically injured as well.

Section 2: Four Types of Bullies

Bully Type 1 – The Disser

>> Facts

- Dissers come in male and female versions, but the methods of girl bullying vary.

- Male dissers more often threaten their victims physically

- Girls tend to taunt them and call them names, or Cyber-bully other students

- Female dissers can also be observed more often as acting like Snobs, Excluders and Ignorers, or Gossips and Rumor Mongers

Bully Type 1 – The Disser

Bully Story

Recently the parents of a former Fayetteville, Arkansas, student filed a law suit against the school district and the administration there, claiming that their son Billy Wolfe was picked on and bullied over and over, and was the subject of sexual harassment. Allegedly, his schoolmates teased him about being gay, which he said he was not, and often called him curse words.

This federal lawsuit, 33 pages in length, alleges that Billy was subjected over and over to cyber bullying on Facebook, among other things.

>> Tips

The most important quality a school needs is to be a place where all students feel safe, respected, and looked after. Justice and fairness have to be the cornerstones, and teachers, counselors, parents, and all other staff must take the lead in providing a safe environment for kids, both physically and emotionally. All children must feel connected in order to have a sense of community.

This process starts by honoring all children and working to increase their self-esteem. Whenever a child's self-esteem is high, the dissers will have less of a negative impact. To do this, make all your students realize that they count. Provide opportunities for all children to be involved not just a select few.

Bully Type 1 – The Disser

>> Strategies

1   *Create a warm, friendly climate in your school where all kids are valued and no bully talk is allowed, by posting lots of pictures of all sorts of kids working together.*

Ask your students:

- How can we make our school friendlier? What little or big changes could be made to make it more welcoming? Then follow through.

2   *Choose a team name for each class or grade and enlist the teams' help in fighting bullying.*

Ask your students:

- Students, from now on we are learning teams. What team name(s) can you suggest? Why? What team colors would be great? Why?

- Ask students to choose the best names/colors, and the use them.

3   *Ask students to compliment a different classmate each day, making sure not to overlook anyone. Ask them for a list of positive, encouraging adjectives such as "helpful," "nice," "friendly," "cheerful," "outstanding," "excellent," etc., post the list on the bulletin board, and encourage students to use them in regards to one another.*

Bully Type 1 – The Disser

4 *Make sure you and other staffers compliment several students each day so that by the end of the week or two weeks, all of them have heard at least one positive comment. Get out this bulletin to the faculty:*

"It is a fact that all of us do better in a positive environment. Therefore, be sure find something to praise when checking a student's homework or test paper."

5 *Test your students to see how much factual information they have about bullies with the help of the bully worksheet on the next page.*

6 *Tell your students that boys and girls often bully differently. How much do they really know about girl bullies? Find out by giving them the Mean Chicks quiz on page 18.*

7 *Designate a "The Bullying Stops Here" teacher and parent committee. Ask for volunteers at the next faculty meeting and Open House.*

- Pass around a sheet with this heading: The Bullying Stops Here Committee. Please sign your name if you have any interest in working on this committee. Not much time is required, only your caring and concern.

- Call a meeting of all people who signed up and have the group volunteer or choose a chair person. Many schools find that having co-chairs—one from the faculty, one from the community—works best.

Section 2: Four Types of Bullies

Bully Worksheet

What is a bully? _____

_____

How can you recognize a bully? _____

_____

Do you know a bully? _____

_____

What have you seen/heard them do? _____

_____

What is a good way of dealing with a bully? _____

_____

What is the best way of dealing with a bully? _____

_____

Have you ever been bullied? Describe the incident. _____

_____

_____

_____

What advice do you have for kids who are bullied? _____

_____

What message do you want to send the bullies? _____

_____

What punishment should a bully receive? _____

_____

Section 2: Four Types of Bullies

Mean Chicks Quiz

1. Can you describe some of the ways that girls are mean? _____

_____

2. Can you tell the difference between minor girl meanness and major girl meanness?

_____

_____

3. Do you know how to deal with and report major girl meanness? _____

_____

4. Do you know any mean-chicks prevention strategies? _____

_____

5. What opportunities are there just for girls to excel? _____

_____

6. How can girls show their leadership? _____

_____

7. How can girls best de-stress? _____

_____

8. What opportunities are there for girls to be honored for their achievements?

_____

Bully Type 1 – The Disser

>> Tips

Especially vulnerable to being dissed are the new kids in school, kids who have been sick, have different names or habits, wear glasses or braces, are skinny, big, tall, short, immigrants, less intelligent or more intelligent, are frail or handicapped, and so forth.

These days, dissing often involves teasing, harassing, or belittling via cell phones, Facebook or MySpace websites. But bullying of all types is reduced drastically if it is taken seriously, just like speeding on the highway.

>> Strategies

8 **Create a Bully Report.**

- Head a sheet up as follows: **BULLY REPORT**. Leave the rest blank for parent/teacher input. Ask for suggestions for the best method to report any bullying at the next Open House or parent/teacher meeting. Set a due date and collect all suggestions. Have the anti-bullying committee go over the suggestions.

9 ***Ask students to design their own samples of a bully reporting form with input from their friends, siblings, and community members.***

- This can also be a class project. Collect all samples and have the committee study them. Choose the top three suggestions and print copies of them.

Bully Type 1 – The Disser

>> Strategies

10 *Yellow, Orange, and Red Bully Alert: Print the forms on yellow paper for a 1st bully report, orange paper for the 2nd time, and red paper for the 3rd report involving the same student.*

- Post these forms in the lobby of the school, in the Media Center/Library and Guidance Department, under the heading: Attention--these forms mean business.

- As a basic rule or set of consequences, require a parent conference for the first report, the loss of a privilege, such as forfeiting a field trip or participation in a class celebration, for a 2nd report, and the required participation in an anger management class for a 3rd report.

11 *Hold a contest for the best anti-bully approach by students. Ask students, teachers and parents to vote on the top choices. Award a prize to the creator of the winning anti-bully approach and get the news out.*

- In addition, send a thank you note to the runners-up: "Thank you for submitting your ideas for an anti-bully approach. Your interest and willingness to help out are much appreciated."

12 *Distribute copies of the forms to the students and staff, and place some in all classrooms, the coaches' office in the gym, the cafeteria, and the parent organizations. Ask that these forms be used at all club meetings, school functions, sporting events, and anywhere else students congregate.*

Bully Type 1 – The Disser

>> Strategies

13   *Work on the actual process of bully reporting next. How are these forms to be submitted to the committee/administration? Ask teachers, students, and parents how these forms are to be delivered. How about setting up a Facebook for students to report the bullying? That type of reporting is more familiar to students and less threatening.*

- One solution is to set up a box like a mail- or suggestion box, into which students can drop their reports about the bullying they observe or personally experience. Have students design such a box, or ask a business to contribute one. Some schools place a box into each wing of the building, however some students will not use these. They don't want to risk their peers seeing them. So, make one available in the Guidance Office as well.

14   *Hold a Bully Drill—send a "fake" bully report through the reporting system and see how long it takes to get to the bully terminators, the Bullying Stops Here Committee. Also, discuss the best location of the box. Can it be placed in such a way that students who report bullying will not get ostracized for "telling" or "tattling" by their classmates?*

- One school designated a locked locker on each hallway, cut a mail slot into it, and instructed the bully reporters to slip in their reports during class time, whenever they got a pass to go the restroom or to return a library book.

15   *Train all staff, including parents and community members as bully spotters and provide them with the appropriate reporting forms. Provide parents with envelopes that are pre-stamped; in other words, no postage due. Ask a civic group if they would like to sponsor the mail-in reports.*

Bully Type 1 – The Disser

>> Strategies

16   *Once the committee, the forms, the precise reporting methods are in place and have been tested, and the punitive rules have been agreed on, post a sign at the school door, the gym, and the sporting venues that says "Welcome to a Bully-free Zone."*

- Ask students, individually or as a club project, to design the sign. Give recognition to the student(s) who came up with the best design. Or rotate the sign to spotlight the different creators of the sign.

>> Tips

Depending on the circumstances, just about any student can be, or may be, dissed at school. But once students have a tried-and-true method to report the verbal or relational bullying instances, and notice the results, the cases of abuse will lessen quickly and drastically.

17   *Ask your students to make a list of all negative or teasing comments about themselves that they have heard in the last six months or a year. Have them rewrite these comments into positive ones and post them at home in their rooms or tape them to their notebooks.*

18   *Ask students to write a paragraph making fun of themselves. Only they are allowed to poke fun at their person, abilities, background, looks, etc. Have them share the paragraphs if they want to. If not, not. For homework, have them write a paper on this topic: The Dumbest (or The Silliest) Thing I've Ever Done.*

Bully Type 1 – The Disser

>> Strategies

19 | *Hold a discussion dealing with biting humor, sarcasm, and witticisms, or have a language arts teacher do so. Hold a stand-up comic contest during which only self-derogatory remarks and jokes are allowed— and nothing negative about another student or person.*

20 | *Discuss the meaning of friendship and real friends. Ask students to research "friendship" on the web. Ask the Media Specialist to provide a list of books dealing with friendship and ask students to read them. List some of the titles here:*

_____

_____

_____

_____

_____

_____

- Ask parents if they want to make a donation to buy some paperbacks dealing with the beauty of friendship.

21 | *Choose the theme of friendship and ask students to think and write about friendship. The friendship worksheet on the next page will get them started.*

Section 2: Four Types of Bullies

Friendship Worksheet

What is the best thing your friends do for you? _____

_____

What is the most fun you've ever had with your friends? Give details. _____

_____

What should you do when your friends want you to pick on, harass, or play a mean trick on another student? _____

_____

Rewrite these statements below, that you can use for excuses, so they make sense to you:

"My mom/dad would ground me like forever if I participated in bullying someone."

"I wish I could pass on this 'funny' message and call another student a name, but I'm already in trouble with my parents."

"I can't pick on anyone 'cause my parents are way strict."

"I'd like to (join in whatever bully acts your peers ask you to) but I'm already in deep trouble."

Memorize three of the above excuses, use them a lot, and tell your friends to use them. Do you have a better excuse for not participating in dissing a classmate? Write it here:

_____

Bully Type 1 – The Disser

QUOTE: Paul R., Guidance Counselor (for 17 years):

"When I first started working in middle school, I used to spend more than half my time counseling either girls who were teased or taunted, or girls who did it. Then I started this new program. Every student signs an "I Will Not Bully" contract that spells out all the different ways that kids disrespect one another and the consequences.

For example, for a first offense, the contract breakers get to have lunch detention with me in my conference room. One time's usually a-plenty. I'm a fun person, but believe me, most kids would rather eat with their best buds than me."

>> Tips

Kids who watch instance after instance of dissing and hateful speech go unreported, unchecked, and unpunished at their school assume this is acceptable behavior.

Once they accept the dissing as everyday behavior, they either imitate it or worse, they will get inured to seeing their classmates in pain and tolerate even more serious forms of bullying.

This acceptance of unfairness and meanness can poison their whole school experience and cause them—in the long run—to lose their humanity. Letting even the lesser forms of bullying go on institutionalizes the crushing and demeaning of the human spirit.

Bully Type 1 – The Disser

>> Strategies

22 *Post messages all over school that remind the student body that all kids deserve respect. Use quotes from your student leaders. Ask the sponsors of the various school clubs/sports teams to ask their students for statements about being respectful and post those direct statements, after getting the students' and their parents' permission, of course.*

23 *What is your school's motto? Examine it and be sure to include the word Respect in it. That also means that we adults can't use anger in teaching, setting up rules, and running the schools. There can be no screaming or cursing administrators, coaches, teachers, or other staff members. Parents must be encouraged to use a respectful tone in the rearing of their kids, as well.*

ACTIVITY

Imaginary tape recorders

- Ask your students to become imaginary tape recorders for a day or a week, and listen to the comments of their classmates without making it obvious they're listening.

- Ask them to write down all harmful comments they hear, not who said it but what was said. Have them also include themselves.

- Ask them to create their own shorthand and reporting system to simplify the process.

- Ask them to make up categories for the various types of hurtful comments they hear, such as derogatory statements about any
  - Smaller and weaker kids
  - Kids from different ethnic groups or speaking with an accent
  - Overweight or underweight kids
  - Less than perfect-looking kids
  - Smarter or slower kids
  - Gay or lesbian kids, and so forth

- Tally the reports. Numbers can tell how wide-spread the dissing and hateful comments are at your school. Teach your students to chart their results.
  - What specific negative comments were the most frequent?
  - What can be done about them?
  - How can all students participate in stopping this kind of hurtful communication?

- Discuss the results of the "Tape Recorder for One Day" activity and praise your students for their work. That makes them participants in your effort to increase your students' self-esteem. Students feel more appreciated when they know that no matter what others may or may not say about them to their faces or behind their backs, they count. They are important, validated, and not to be dissed. That tendency will lessen the more students see one another as valuable human beings and realize that they have the power to improve the school climate.

Bully Type 1 – The Disser

>> Strategies

24 Bring a few cans or boxes of food to school and discuss the labeling of products, including clothes. Have students design their own products and think of catchy labels. Compare and contrast this labeling exercise with the stereotyping of human beings by teaching your kids about the huge number of nations in the world. Have students research some unusual-for-them countries and report on the special contributions of these countries.

25 Tie this exercise to your students' own backgrounds and have them "advertise" something special about their individual ethnicity or heritage. Students believe that they matter if they feel they do to you. To increase their feelings of self-worth even more, use the worksheet on the next page.

- Use these facts in a "**Who Am I**" quiz game show.

- Ask students to interview one another for 10 minutes, pretending to be members of the paparazzi.

- Then play the game, reading only the answer to one of the questions and ask the students to guess whose answer this was.

- The more your students know about their classmates, the more they realize their commonalities. This realization provides a protective mantel for all of them, which discourages other kids from dissing them.

Section 2: Four Types of Bullies

Self-worth Worksheet

Where and when were you born? _____

_____

What were the circumstances of your birth, according to what your mother, father, or other relatives told you? _____

_____

What's your first memory? Give details. _____

_____

What was the first house or apartment like in which you lived? _____

_____

Who looked after you when you were little and what do you remember about them? _____

_____

What was your favorite food back then? _____

_____

What was your favorite toy back then? _____

_____

What was your favorite TV show or song back then? _____

_____

What was the worst thing that happened to you back then? _____

_____

Have you gone back to the place of your birth since then, if you have moved, or, if you haven't, what has changed in that place since then? _____

_____

Whom do you count on now when you're in trouble? _____

_____

Bully Type 1 – The Disser

>> Strategies

26 *Use the worksheet facts as a resource in designing an <u>Anti-bully Tin Board</u>. Cut out tags with student names, tack them on the board, and run strings from the names to the various places on a world map where the students' ancestors might have come from. You can assign colors to certain countries so students can see who else has that same color or ethnic background.*

- Have students research the most famous man or woman (be it a politician, athlete, artist, or author) or the most famous work of art, or invention, achievement, marvel of nature, or architecture related to their place of birth, background or heritage, and draw or copy a picture of this outstanding person, place, or thing. Post the results next to the students' names, so that—by association—the students can feel more pride in their background, plus a heightened self-worth.

- Once students feel appreciated for who they are and where they come from, they are more likely to bond with one another and with the school leaders. If reinforced frequently, this bond can break down the barriers between them and their teachers and staff. As a result they will feel freer to inform you any time their feelings have been hurt because of their peers' disrespect.

27 *Offer students an incentive to make progress in dissing the dissing and getting a handle on hate speech. Give a reward to the class or grade level with the fewest reported dissing complaints, such as free ice cream, a longer lunch time, or an outing to a movie. Ask students what they consider an appropriate reward—no, a new car is not an option!—and provide it.*

- Once students realize they are members of a wonderful class or group all working toward a common goal—stamping out any disrespectful talk or messages among them—they will become verbal bullying preventers.

Bully Type 1 – The Disser

>> Strategies

28 *Have students write skits that focus on intentional dissing versus unintentional dissing. Students can also write scenarios that highlight good-natured teasing versus mean-spirited teasing. Learning to distinguish between a fun pun and an intended slight is important. The students themselves are the best judges. If they feel they are being dissed, they certainly are!*

- Not all students are equally sensitive, however. Those who grow up in large families, or with many brothers, or with parents who tease a lot, may be able to overlook, or even welcome, some teasing. Some parents use humorous teasing in their parenting style. Inform them that kids don't know the boundaries of good-natured teasing, so they need to be taught how to interact with one another in an acceptable manner.

- Have students perform skits to the student body during a Bully Awareness week or month.

QUOTE: Melissa Y., Parent of Five (ages 5 to 21):

 I nip any teasing and "picking" in the bud before it can get out of hand. How? With my trusty calendar on the fridge. The teaser or the child picking on another has got to go a week without TV, cell phone, video games, and computer privileges. In my experience, it takes less than no time at all to get the point across, even with the most hard-headed of my kids. Because after the week comes a whole month of no privileges--none. That hurts!

- So, talking about what kinds of messages are hurtful is key, and having consequences.

- To get your students to be even more open and share their feelings, use the "Your Feelings Matter" worksheet on the next page.

Your Feelings Matter Worksheet

What makes you...

sad? _____

scared? _____

angry? _____

feel dissed? _____

happy? _____

contented? _____

feel strong? _____

feel important? _____

feel confident? _____

want to do your best? _____

feel determined to do great things? _____

Bully Type 1 – The Disser

>> Strategies

- On the Anti-Bully Tin Board, post the names of students and the great things they wish to accomplish some day. Explain that true greatness requires not only doing great things for the world to see but also treating others with respect and having good character traits that may not be seen outwardly.

29 *Ask students to come up with a list of nouns describing good character and have them advertise these good character traits on mobiles made out of construction paper to hang from the ceiling in the classroom or lobby. Get them started with this list: Honesty, Loyalty, Acceptance… Ask them to complete this list.*

30 *Make an RAK journal: Ask students to keep a record of all Random Acts of Kindness, or signs of friendship they observe at school and in the community. Help them to begin by asking them to copy these words, then fill in the rest.*

The nicest thing I have seen someone doing was…

QUOTE: Fred J., High school teacher (for 31 years)

" From the moment my students step in my room, I work on building support among each and every one of them. I treat them all with the utmost respect and expect them to do the same. That's why I give each student two grades—one for their mastery of the subject (for their report card), the other one on their character development (in the form of a note). I notice how they talk to each other, help each other out, and so forth. Any time I hear some bully talk by any of my kids, that's it. I have them see me after school, just like if they were failing. Then I assign them make-up work—a written report on a non-bullying book, things like that. "

Bully Type 1 – The Disser

>> Strategies

31 *Make a Gratitude Box: Ask your students to design a reporting form for the positive actions they notice and designate a way to recognize the many good citizens in your school. Install this gratitude box, similar to a bully-reporting box, for acting-good reports. The same box, or a different one, can be used.*

- Encourage everyone, including the cafeteria and maintenance staff, to participate.

- Each day, a new name can then be pulled from the submitted names, and the winning student can be announced over the intercom.

- The more positive touches of recognition that the students receive, the less often will they turn to dissing for attention. This is not an overnight process, but can be a gradual change in the vulture culture that permeates too many of our schools like a toxic gas. Work on creating a victors' mindset. Only then can a bully school turn into a beneficent school.

DISCUSSION QUESTIONS

1. Most teachers, parents, and law enforcement officers think that when serious verbal bullying erupts in school, it is caused by boys. In fact, male students dominate in the number of discipline referral slips. Is that true in your school? Do the girls in your school really bully less often or are they just more subtle about it, and therefore don't get caught as much?

2. Research proves that involved dads produce kids who are less likely to bully, be it with words or deeds. Yet male teachers are far outnumbered by female teachers, meaning few male role models exist in our society where many boys come from single mom- or grandmother-led homes. What can be done about that? How can more male role models become part of your school routine?

3. Male aggressive tendencies have begun to rub off on females. Girls are now beginning to imitate the behavior of boys, yet picking up only their worst traits, rather than their best conduct. What can be done to reverse this trend and to influence girls to concentrate more on their own best potentials and possibilities?

Bully Type 2 – The Hitter

Insight

The hitter is a bully who physically attacks another student and stands several perilous rungs above the disser or mean-word mouther on the bully severity scale. That does not mean all dissers automatically escalate into hitters, but many do. They may begin with just a touch of physical violence but once they have crossed the line from verbal to physical bullying, they can continue on until they inflict serious bodily harm. And even if the bodily harm is just a little shove into the lockers or a push into the Dumpster—without obvious lasting scars—the psychological wounds may be severe and life-long. What one student can shrug off, another carries around with him/her for decades.

Bullying behavior that expresses itself in hitting starts early, often in kindergarten or 1st and 2nd grade. Too often, however, that early hitting and punching are overlooked without someone doing something about it. Yet if kids get away with even small incidents of physical aggression, they grow bolder and more menacing. Until recently it was mostly boys who were the "designated" hitters, designated by circumstances in which they felt free to slap another kid because they feel inferior and wanted to appear superior.

In fact, many boys can suffer from low esteem. For example, if their reading ability is compared to that of girls', many boys cannot compete in the early grades because boys usually learn to read more slowly than girls. To counteract their feeling of not being as "smart" as girls, many boys try to make themselves feel better by putting down the smallest, smartest, or least-able-to-defend himself boy in their vicinity.

Boys also seem to be at another disadvantage in many school systems. For example, in the diagnoses of emotionally disturbed students, boys outnumber girls three to one. The same can be true for kids classified as special education or special needs students.

In contrast, girls are more verbal from early on, so they may not only read better but also write better, starting with 1st grade. This ability makes girls capable of expressing their bullying instincts more readily with language. At least they have that outlet and can share their frustrations by talking or writing about them, if given the chance to channel them properly.

Boys, however, use fewer words, have a smaller vocabulary, and often hide their feelings. Boys don't cry, is their motto. Yet their anger and frustration need some type of outlet as well. At the same time, they grow faster and bigger physically, which—mixed with their frustration, low self-esteem, and a willingness to resort to fists, knives, and even guns—can lead to horrible results.

Bully Type 2 – The Hitter

Thus, we have to understand the differences and motivations of boy hitters and girl hitters and address all of them. We need programs for all violent-prone kids, such as anger management courses that teach them techniques to let off steam. Boys, as well as girls, need to learn how to vent their emotions in socially acceptable ways. Often having boys work in boy pairs in class can lower the competitive aspect. Also, telling girls that we are aware of the changing culture and want to help them find other productive solutions to their anger and frustration is useful.

>> Tips

Signs of hitter bullies on the loose include the following behaviors that can be observed in many school buildings and school yards:
- **Destroying another student's property**
- **Shoving, cutting in line, or clothes- or hair pulling**
- **Punching, elbowing, or tripping a fellow student**
- **Beating up another student**
- **Videotaping a beating or a fight, and posting it on line or through cell phones.**

The last-mentioned incarnation of bullying is the most recent one and often has traumatic consequences.

Bully Type 2 – The Hitter

Bully Story

One of the most infamous incidents of bullies hitting a classmate was the one involving a 16-year old Mulberry High School cheerleader. As recorded on a video broadcast nationally, she was jumped by six girls, ranging in age from 14 to 17, and beaten severely. According to the Sheriff's Office in Lakeland, Fl, the victim suffered a huge bump near her left eye, a concussion, and possible damage to a tooth. She knew her assailants who not only attacked her but also video recorded the assault and later posted it on the Internet.

This physical bullying incident was supposedly incited by some comments the victim had made on line. The hitters carried out their planned assault off the school grounds, yet the roots most likely lay in the school environment that did not stop these teens from carrying out their extreme aggression.

>> Strategies

Encourage targets of bullies to get help and not to hesitate, but never tell the physically bullied kids just to stand up for themselves. It is useless. They have either done that already, or it didn't work. Neither does saying "Stop it!" by a spectator end the hitting--for long.

- Words and repeated warnings fall on deaf ears once the bullying has reached the beating stage.

- Admonishing a hitter or hit squad may cause them to simply change locations and choose to take their physical aggression off the school grounds, but it doesn't prevent the hitting.

Bully Type 2 – The Hitter

>> Strategies

33

Prepare a list of immediate and meaningful consequences for the slightest incident of physical aggression. Make these consequences known to every student and parent, and have students and parents sign a note that proves they are aware of the consequences.

- File these notes. Periodically review these notes, so that you will remember who in your school population may be a potential hitter and keep them under radar.

34

Use a "hot-line" reporting system by phone or e-mail that informs you and/or the administration immediately of the threat of a physical bullying before the fact. Also, a chart with the names of teachers/administrators who will drop everything and step in immediately needs to be made available to each child and parent.

35

Designate a Go-To Adult. Brainstorm with student leaders, grade chairmen and –women, and master teachers as to what must be done at the first hint or inkling of a fight possibly breaking out on the school grounds or off it. Designate one faculty member on each hall to be the Go-To Adult. This adult needs to know how to defuse students' escalating tensions before it's too late.

36

Encourage all students to use their creativity to get the no-fighting message across. Ask them to write a school song including a bully-free message and short stories in which a big bully reforms. A positive climate, consistency, and sharing bully-prevention lesson plans and tension-lessening hints/ideas work well.

- Always ask student leaders to get involved in the anti-bully work and ask for their best suggestions.

Bully Type 2 – The Hitter

>> Tips

Empirical research proves that hitters often receive little attention at home or are raised by controlling parents. In either case, they have not been taught self-control and the basic rules of good behavior. Often there is no one in their lives who cares enough to teach them how to act without physically lashing out. Any early misbehavior along those lines is often swept under the rug, excused, or dealt with via a slap.

Also these days, Reality TV shows, music, video games, and movies encourage the bullies to think that physical bullying is acceptable or even extolled. When kids are overexposed to violence in the media, they tend to react more violently themselves. But physical bullying tendencies can be stopped by:

- *Teaching kids to respect the rights of other kids and their property*
- *Swiftly punishing all instances of physical bullying and "messing with" other kids' or their siblings' belongings*
- *Taking away meaningful privileges, that means consequences "with teeth," at the first sign of physical bullying*
- *The best anti-bully-dote is consistent rule enforcement that makes the hitter think twice before he/she hits another kid again. Fortunately we have made enormous progress in stopping the hitters. It is best to catch all potential hitters before they beat up a classmate, when they are still in the threatening stage. In this, we have the best assistants any bully proofer could have. We need to recognize them, train them, and then let them go to work.*

The same school that has a hitter in its midst also has a group of bully terminators, and the ratio of hitter to bully terminator is enormous. For every "toughie," as one mother close to the beaten-up Florida cheerleader called the girl hitters, there may be as many as 20 or more determined bully fight preventers at school. Inform the whole student body that their help in overcoming the bullies is needed. You do that by:

- *Having open discussions and journal writing for in-class assignments on why kids fight*
- *Giving homework assignments to check to see if students understand their importance in reporting the threat of, and putting a stop to, any physical aggression by a bully*

Bully Type 2 – The Hitter

>> Strategies

37 *Many students are asked to hand in a major written project during their school experience. Include in the list of possible topics the subject of "school bullies." Have students research the best anti-bully approaches used in the schools in their home state. Have them compare the methods practiced in other schools to those implemented in their school.*

38 *Inform the media in your community about your effort and have them be co-sponsors of your anti-bully campaign. The press can set aside space for the best "no more bullies" essays of your students.*

- Use some of the ideas of the worksheet on the next page to get your students engaged in writing about school bullies.

39 *Give a monetary or other reward to students who promptly report the threat of a student on the verge to resort to physical bullying, just like many crime-stopping groups offer a financial incentive to catch the criminals.*

- Find a business in the community to match the reward.

- A bank could be asked to start a small college-savings account in the names of the helpful kids.

Section 2: Four Types of Bullies

Prevent Fighting Worksheet

Write a skit in which a student threatens to beat up another student. Explain how verbal bullying might have lead up to the threat and how this conflict can be resolved peacefully.

_____

_____

_____

Write down three things students should think about before they get involved in fighting.

a) _____

b) _____

c) _____

Why do you think so many people like to watch kids fight and how can you make them stop?

_____

_____

What should a friend of the fighter say to de-escalate the potentially violent situation? Give three examples.

a) _____

b) _____

c) _____

If you could post one rule about kids' not fighting in every school in the US, what would it be?

_____

Bully Type 2 – The Hitter

>> Strategies

40 Check the call buttons (often called panic buttons) installed in each classroom/hallway and make sure they work. Add some call buttons at several other points around campus to be used to inform the administration of a fight about to break out.

41 Hold a practice drill, just like you have a tornado or fire drill, to rehearse what is to be done immediately in case of physical bullying, such as sequestering the bully and holding him/her until the ensuing strict consequences kick in. All physical bullying must be dealt with severely.

42 Set up a <u>bully pen</u>, a special room, a decked-out closet, or a secluded corner in the main office or Resource Officer's room, where the hitter can be isolated, given his/her assignments, and held for lunch detention or until his/her parents come. Have them go through some anger management strategies while in there.

43 Periodically recheck your school's readiness to swiftly deal with the physical bullies, not only males but also females. Use the worksheet on the next page to raise the awareness of girls who bully physically.

- A zero physical bullying policy must be enforced not only at school but also at related school events and on the bus.

Worksheet

Girl Bullies Worksheet

Check the correct type of mean girl behavior for each. Talk about the best way to deal with each type of bullying.

	THE SNOB	GOSSIP	TEASER	HITTER	TRAITOR
Punching, pinching, or tripping somebody at school, on the bus or at the bus stop					
Mean video- or picture phoning or forwarding, including those done anonymously					
Taunting, oral or text insults, including making fun of another girl's clothes, shoes, or bag					
Rumor spreading and gossiping					
Ignoring or leaving a girl out of a school activity/event, on purpose					
Spilling a drink on another girl's work, notebook, or project					
Trash talking, ridiculing, or mean facial expressions					
Pretending, or lying, or telling secrets					
Ruining someone's clothes, vandalizing her things, or her parent's mailbox					
Ganging up with other girls and beating up a student					

Bully Type 2 – The Hitter

>> Strategies

44 *Make sure all students have a few hitting-report slips in their backpacks to fill out and drop into a collection box on the bus. These can be like the verbal bully reports, which can have a checklist for the various bully acts, or they can be different forms. Bus drivers need to turn in any of these reports promptly, in addition to writing up their own statements.*

45 *Involve the physical bully's parents immediately, without delay. Contact them directly and inform them of the bully behavior, the consequence, and the escalating punishment, should the bully behavior continue. While the first bully responders are the students, the second bully responders are the parents and teachers.*

46 *Plan ahead for any misreporting of bullies or any student claiming "I was just joking" when he/she submits the name of a bully who isn't one. Spell out the consequences for this false reporting in the student hand book, right along with the serious consequences for bullying.*

Bully Type 2 – The Hitter

47

All parents, not only the moms and dads of the bullies, need to be engaged in the bully fighting. Initiate the formation of a special PTA group or other teacher-parent committee to deal with bully fighting only. Have the parents of the hitters be part of the process. Getting them involved will encourage them to discourage physical violence in their sons/daughters.

QUOTE:

Carla V., Single Mom of three and PTA Member (kids ages 12, 14, and 15)

 Don't forget about sibling rivalry, okay? It's a form of bullying too. I've got no use for it—none. When one of my kids gets picked on by their sibling, I take away the allowance of the guilty one. Fairness has got to start at home, so the brother/sister that got teased or picked on or punched gets the allowance I held back.

- Ask your school's No-More-Bullies Committee to gather the best anti-bully practices from around the country. The members or the chair can search the web. Next, they can e-correspond with schools that have few or no bully problems and with those that have many and start a school alert system—a bully bulletin that gets sent out electronically to every parent. So all parents are informed on the effort to end bullying now.

- This group can also tally the incidents of bullying in your school system and pinpoint where and when most bully incidents occur and why.

Bully Type 2 – The Hitter

>> Strategies

48

Periodically review the consequences for the bullies and, depending on the grade level, consider adding the following forms of consequences, as are appropriate:
- *losing privileges and any free time for a short or longer time*
- *losing recess privileges*
- *losing a school parking permit (for high schoolers)*
- *losing bus transportation*
- *denying bullies access to the driver's ed classes that are required before the permit is issued*

- The **Anti-Bully Tin board**, mentioned previously, needs to feature prominently the different categories for bullying and the escalating consequences. Again, this works best with the student body involved. As many students as possible can be tasked with creating an anti-bully chart that also needs to go into every classroom for display.

- Be sure the bullying offenses are grouped into categories of severity and include
   - Minimal bullying, starting with teasing and going on to name-calling and taunting, all falling under the dissing category and including Techno Bullying in all its forms and disguises

   - Physical bullying, such as pinching, shoving, "accidental" elbowing, door slamming; in other words, bullying that goes beyond the verbal and texting kind and involves another person's property, plus hitting, fighting, or causing physical harm otherwise

   - Most severe criminal behavior, such as serious threats (also those communicated or in code on Facebook, or web pages, etc.), and/or involving weapons, and banding together with other students for the purpose of demeaning, intimidating, or hurting others, etc.

- An Anti-Bully Tin Board in the lobby works best if one or two main people—a counselor, social worker, resource officer, or assistant principal, for example—are in charge. With the involvement of the students, this person can also post a log/chart of the "Bully No More" progress. What decrease in bully reporting has been observed?

Bully Type 2 – The Hitter

>> Strategies

49 *Ask the student council to set up a contest as to which grade level has the fewest bully referrals in a given month. A reward—such as extra lunch time, free time, a no-homework pass for a day—can be given to the grade that wins. "And the winners are…"*

50 *Reward individual bully-pattern breakers. Utilize and train these students as Peer Helpers or mentors for younger students who are bullies. Keep the parents informed of all positive changes. Document the improvement step by step. Connect the parents of the reformed bully with those of students in need of reform, so they can share success tips. "This is what worked for my child…"*

51 *For stubborn physical bullies who have a record of hitting other kids more than once, write out an IBP—an Individual Bully-Preventing plan—and forward copies to teachers and parents, and on to the next grade levels. Too many bullies revert to their anti-social behavior once they change schools or grade levels. Pair these students up with a school based or community based mentor.*

52 *Design a bully-alert system for the student's future teachers. Too often, hard-core hitters have other school problems as well and skip around from school to school, or move out of state. But a note attached to the student's permanent record informing the receiving school of the kid's prior bully problem can help. Student health challenges may not be completely overcome, but bullying is a disease that can be cured—now.*

Bully Type 2 – The Hitter

>> Strategies

53 *Start a system-wide method of bully reporting, so all parents can be informed not only as to which schools produce top scholars but also what their bully factor is. What is the percentage of bully incidents in this elementary or middle school or high school versus that one?*

- And what bully-stopping programs do they have/offer?

- Have this information available up front and at the beginning of the school year.

54 *Physical bullies are often masters in excuses and champions in denials, unless caught red-handed. Ask the PTA or a business to purchase some tape recorders and video cams, to be available for teachers and teacher aides to document any bully behavior.*

55 *Expand your school's anti-bully program by starting an Intervention Program for any grade levels or classrooms that have frequent physical aggression reports. This program should focus on requiring the hitters to:*
- *learn to examine their physical actions*
- *be able to tell whom they hurt*
- *analyze why they did what they did*
- *take the consequences, and*
- *develop a plan to get what they want in an acceptable way in the future*

Bully Type 2 – The Hitter

>> Tips

The hitters share the same nature and traits that the lesser bullies have, although their aggressive tendencies express themselves much more damagingly. Hitters also:

- *Want to dominate other kids*
- *Act selfishly and are most concerned about themselves*
- *Pick their "prey" based on who is smaller, different, more friendless, smarter, or more popular than they are*
- *Don't accept responsibility for their actions unless forced to*
- *Desperately desire attention and instant fame, no matter how much they have to hurt others*

Of course, not all hitters are the same. Some have more than, or several of, the above traits; others fewer, but they all have negative feelings toward many of their peers.

>> Long-term Effects

In their own way, the hitters are calling out for help. They want to be stopped and taught how to increase their standing and popularity without having to beat up other kids. A recent <u>Newsweek</u> article states that studies on teen popularity prove that popular kids more frequently:

- *Reach out to others*
- *Make fun things happen or participate in projects*
- *Give compliments to other kids*

Bully Type 2 – The Hitter

>> Strategies

56 | *Teach your students the acceptable ways to become more popular and to get known around school. One example is by helping others. Make sure all your kids have the chance to do some good. Get them thinking about doing that with the worksheet on the following page.*

- Hand a one-dollar bill of play money to students and ask them to imagine they have only one dollar and want to put it to the best use possible.

57 | *Ask each student who can to bring in a few cents. Once you have collected one dollar, discuss with your students what they think should be done with it to do the most good. Have one student step up to the board and record all valid suggestions. Then take a vote and send the $1 on its beneficial way.*

58 | *Get your students to come up with some school rules that encourage other kids to do good deeds. Use the worksheet on page 52 to make your students think about others more often and to become more unselfish.*

>> Tips

TEEN/TWEEN EMPOWERMENT
By removing the "allure" for kids to bully and by pointing them into another direction—the caring one—we can empower them. Emphasizing important values is key. We do that by connecting every kid to a cause. These causes may be school- or community-related.

Section 2: Four Types of Bullies

Doing Good Worksheet

Imagine you have only one dollar and want to put it to the best use possible.
(Write at least three ideas for each.)

How could you help a baby with just one dollar?

_____

_____

How could you help a desperately sick person with just one dollar?

_____

_____

How could you help another nation with just one dollar?

_____

_____

How could you save someone's life with just one dollar?

_____

_____

What good could you do if you had a thousand friends each wanting to contribute one dollar?

_____

_____

What would you tell others to get them to join you in your efforts?

_____

_____

What would you do if you had a million dollars just for the purpose of doing some good?

_____

_____

If you could, what percentage would you keep back for yourself and your family and why?

_____

_____

What good would you do for another nation if you had the chance? Name this nation and tell why.

_____

_____

Section 2: Four Types of Bullies

End the Bullying Worksheet

Have you ever watched someone act mean to another person? What happened?

_____

_____

How did you react and why?

_____

_____

If you could write a school rule against mean behavior, what would this rule say?

_____

If you could give a big reward for niceness, what would you call it, and what would it consist of?

_____

_____

List three examples of when you were nice to someone.

a) _____

b) _____

c) _____

How do you feel when you do something nice?

_____

_____

Describe what you can do today for somebody that is a nice gesture.

_____

_____

What can you do tomorrow or next week that is nice or unselfish?

_____

What would happen if everyone you know would suddenly do lots of nice things?

_____

Bully Type 2 – The Hitter

>> Strategies

59 *Ask your students to text only good comments and encouraging messages to one another, starting now, or for a limited time, as an experiment. Encourage them to solve problems for themselves and for others, and to tutor others, and be friends, and not detractors.*

60 *Students who have a tendency to be hitters can be taught to manage their anger if the consequences of not doing so are steep. Enroll every student who has physically bullied another or has threatened to do so in an anger management class that cuts into their free or fun time.*

61 *In every school there may be one or two bullies who have relational aggression problems that go much deeper than just dissing and hitting someone once or twice. In that case:*

- *Keep a careful log of what you observe, or hear, about the incorrigible bullies*
- *Keep this information in a separate file*
- *Pass copies of this information on to the counselor, school nurse, school psychologist, resource officer, and principal and make sure consequences are in place*
- *A month later, make sure these bullies or "scary" kids, as they are sometimes called, have not fallen through the cracks*
- *A year later, check on these scary kids again. Untreated physical bullies can cause irreparable harm down the road*

Bully Type 2 – The Hitter

>> Tips

If you don't step in, the hitters feel like nobody cares. They may get depressed and sink deeper and deeper into depression, always hoping for someone to help them and not getting it. Eventually they may turn into hardened criminals.

A similar state of mind can affect the bully victims. They too can feel depressed, even though they haven't done anything wrong, and they desperately and seriously need your help. If you do not intervene, both groups can resort to violence. Certainly both groups do less than fulfill their potential because they're engaged in the relational tangle of either hurting their peers or of being hurt by them.

Similar to child abuse, sexual harassment, racism, or rape—the person with more power hurts the one with less power. To simplify, the hitter kid hits the weaker kid. Therefore, we must give the powerless kids more power and punish the abuser of power by disarming him/her.

Most people agree that three groups are involved in the bully problem—the bully, the bullied, and the spectators, and that all three need to get a message:

- *The bullies need the message that bullying stops as of this moment.*

- *The bullied kids need to learn this: "Help is here. All I have to do is turn to the pros—report the incident to the resource officer, a teacher, coach, counselor, or a parent."*

- *Spectators need to know that silence is an encourager. It's like applauding bad behavior, like standing up and cheering for rudeness, meanness, and cruelty. Anyone who does that is a co-bully. So go get help--now.*

Once the spectators move beyond being co-bullies, a new group enters the bully arena—the bully enders or bully terminators.

The Bully-No-More Skit

- Cut out construction paper slips, enough for your enrollment, and label one fourth of the slips BULLY, the second fourth BULLIED, the third fourth SPECTATOR, and the last fourth BULLY TERMINATOR. Turning the slips over, have each student choose one, and get into groups of four, making sure each label is represented. Ask each group of students to write a three-minute skit, using all four characters. Have them act out the skits. The best-anti-bullying skit gets not only the best grade but also a chance to have their skit performed for the entire grade level or school. Why not ask a business or a civic organization to sponsor a cash prize for the best skit?

- Students will write a song, a rap, or commercial about the topic of name calling, taunting, and fighting and their negative impact. They will present their work to the rest of the class who will vote for the best effort. The top ten songs, raps, or commercials will be shared with the rest of the school.

- Hold a poster contest about bullying and display the entries around the school and community. Many banks and other institutions of business will be delighted to sponsor the contest and offer prizes. Parents or students from other schools can be the judges.

- Hold an assembly to inform your students that physical bullying is often associated with other negative behaviors or actions. Contact <u>Bullycide</u>, a national program that shows a video of different kids who committed suicide because of being bullied. This can be shown with a follow-up discussion. As part of the assembly, hand out the following worksheet, and have students complete it anonymously.

> ## >> Tips
>
> *Tell your students that even if their home life is not the best, they can rise above it. They can win out over any minus points of their circumstances. Every time they bite their tongue or restrain their fists, they are winning the battle.*
>
> *Besides teaching your kids to get themselves under better control, help them to develop their empathy muscles. That means every day they should spend a few minutes thinking of others and putting themselves in their shoes. Set the stage for your students' practicing being concerned about others by using the Empathy worksheet.*

Section 2: Four Types of Bullies

Are You A Potential Physical Bully?

Worksheet

	YES	NO
Do you have outbursts of anger or big mood swings?		
Have you ever skipped school, or been suspended, or been in serious trouble?		
Do you have little contact with, or supervision by, your parents or grandparents?		
Do you like to watch violent videos or violent movies, or play violent games, or listen to violent music, or read about violence?		
Do you like to curse, threaten other kids, hit them, or call them names?		
Do you like guns, knives, or other weapons, or are you interested in making bombs?		
Have you been bullied or abused at home?		
Do you have few or no friends, and nobody else who cares about you?		
Is there somebody you really want to get back at?		

Section 2: Four Types of Bullies

Worksheet

Empathy Worksheet

If you could write a letter to someone who was impacted by, or a victim of, youth violence, what would you write? (Use the back of this sheet.)

_____

_____

_____

If you could talk to the young person/s who perpetrated the violence, what would you say?

_____

_____

_____

If you could contact the people closest to the violent perpetrators, what would you tell them?

_____

_____

_____

What new measures have you seen being put in place to reduce youth violence?

_____

_____

_____

Do you think that in the future there will be more youth violence in this country or less? Why?

_____

_____

_____

Why do you think that incidents of youth violence occur more frequently in the US than in other countries?

_____

_____

Bully Type 2 – The Hitter

>> Facts and Questions

- The reason for kids bullying each other with their fists is simple. Nothing serious happens to them. Besides, the problem of physical abuse by kids on kids is seriously underreported. Yet the numbers are staggering. One well-known research study on bullying, commonly known as "Craig and Pepler's Playground Observation," reports that an incident of bullying occurs every seven minutes but only in 4% of cases an adult steps in, while only in 11% of the cases other kids intervene. So we must increase the adult interference and teach kids to insist that adults interfere. How can that be accomplished?

- Bully behavior can spread up and down the ranks. If teachers and other adults allow themselves be bullied by dictatorial administrators, co-workers, or parents, they tend to become less effective and caring, and their students will pick up on that. Too often job burnout is caused by bully supervisors. What can be done to bully proof the faculty, staff, and parents?

- The recent focus on scholastic upgrading at all costs has caused more and more teachers and administrators to turn a blind eye to bully behavior. But overlooking the bullies can poison a school culture. Is your school so concerned with achievement test scores that it overlooks the bullying? What can be done about it?

>> Tips

A tradition of bullying in a school will cause this bad behavior to be accepted and eventually become institutionalized. Before long then, a bullying hierarchy develops and students pass on the bully train of thought and conduct to younger kids, just like other honored school traditions are passed on.

Sadly, this sick culture can give rise to an even more dangerous type of bully.

Bully Type 3 – The Controller

Insight

The controller is a bully who is several rungs up from the disser and a crucial big step up from the hitter in the escalating severity of bully behavior. Both the disser and the hitter rely mainly on opportunity as an ally and often act alone. If a smaller, weaker, or less attractive kid just happens to come along, they pounce. But if no opportunity presents itself, the "lesser" bullies are less likely to act out. Their weapons, be they words or fists, tend to make their appearance more random and on the sly, and often with little group behavior involved.

In contrast, the controllers are often schemers and more likely to plan ahead. They want to control their prey to such a degree that they aim to dominate, direct, and regulate their victim's actions in a tactical and overwhelming manner that is always negative. That means they strategize ahead of time when and where the best chances are for their chosen prey to show up unprotected or unsupervised. And then they strike, and how.

Some controller bullies do work alone, focus on just one victim, stalk him/her, and make life miserable for one innocent kid. That type of stalking can be subtle or it can go beyond just following the victim around in the school hallway and harassing him/her. It can actually escalate into a fixation and include every aspect of the victim's life.

However much worse is when the control bully exerts influence on similar-minded kids and attracts a large group of domineering kids that are all out to prey on any unsuspecting kids, or at least those compliant enough to keep quiet. Therefore, the controllers start by controlling their buddies, or followers, first. Once they get them involved in some minor bully behavior, they entice them along into more serious bully actions.

Thus, a control bully group can cause immeasurable harm because the negative behavior of the alpha bully can exponentially increase the bully potential of the members of the bully herd. As a result, the bullied kids don't just have to face one nasty bully. They have to face a horrible hail of bullies.

Bully Type 3 – The Controller

Bully Story

DAMAGED FOREVER

Not long ago, a controlling bully group's outrageous behavior came into the national spotlight.

At Sunnyvale Middle School near Dallas, a large group of the 8th grade boys was involved in something so ugly it boggles the mind. While the whole school seemingly hummed along, it wasn't just one or two isolated big kids who bullied one or two smaller children. Here it was a widespread, almost daily occurrence that involved a huge number of students and lasted for a long time.

What the older boys did was wait around until the academic classes were over for the day, and a lot of kids reported to the gym for P.E. or similar activities. That's when the 8th graders trapped many of the 7th grade boys and threw them to the ground. While the frightened victims screamed, the older students held the younger ones down and threatened to hurt them.

The lead bully would even go so far as to brandish a plastic object at the petrified victims. Meanwhile a boisterous crew would crowd around, applaud, and make disgusting noises. This happened many, many times and not far away from the coaches' offices.

Rod Dreher, a reporter writing for the Dallas Morning News, who covered this story, recalled his own year of being bullied in middle school. Even many years later, he still remembered the pain and outrage of a long-ago incident, when he was 14 and a group of bullies tried to pull his pants off. His harassment lasted for two years, and this demeaning event hovered over him like a permanent storm cloud for decades.

Eventually this type of bullying was stopped but by then the damage had been done.

Bully Type 3 – The Controller

>> Strategies

62 *Examine the reasons for the various different groups, cliques, and clubs in your school, even the informal ones, by asking each group to complete a survey that asks what cliques exist in their school. Students don't have to put their name on the survey. Sometimes, what seems like a harmless bunch of friends hanging out is actually a gang made up of a controlling bully and his/her buds.*

- Even Michael Phelps, an Olympic swimmer, was bullied. After he received his eight gold medals at the 2008 Olympics in China, he admitted that when he was younger, a group of other boys would make fun of him, throw his visor hat out of the bus window, and flick his ears. He recounted these incidents many years after the fact, proving that bully experiences linger like deep scars. Many other famous people also experienced bullying. For example, Victoria Beckham is quoted in the September 22, 2008 edition of <u>Us Magazine</u>: "People would push me around, say they would beat me up… My whole schooling (was) miserable…"

63 *Keep in check all girl cliques. Leaders of mean chick cliques resort more often to non-physical bullying than boys but they do incredible harm as well. They may force girls to run errands for them and do their dirty work. If the top mean chick is into hazing the newest members of the group, that can have more of a psychological component than a physical one, so be on the alert and dig deep.*

64 *Call a meeting of all club presidents, clique top chicks, and team captains and offer them leadership training. Controlling bullies are leaders who are horribly misdirected. Teach them to use their talents in a positive way. Show them what true leadership really is.*

Bully Type 3 – The Controller

>> Strategies

65 *Involve the members of your community's civic and faith-based organizations. Ask them to speak to your students about service projects and worthwhile causes, and then get the various student groups involved in volunteering. Praise the efforts.*

66 *Ask your students what the worst punishment is that could be given to them. What would really hurt them? Would it be it losing the use of one's cell phone? Or not getting to use one's computer? Or having an early curfew? Compile a list of all suggested consequences and check into the legalities of them.*

- At the Open House, share that list with parents, ask for their input, and ask for volunteers to serve on a parent-teacher committee to deal with any potential group bullies who can terrorize a whole school community.

- Have the committee decide on what consequence is appropriate for collective, controlling bullying.

67 *Form an inter-club council with a representative from every school group, clique, club, and athletic team. This club's main agenda is to bully proof all extra-curricular activities which could be used to subtly or openly cause group bullying.*

Bully Type 3 – The Controller

QUOTE: John S., Middle School Teacher (for 24 years)

 On the first day of school I explain my rules. Number one: Be polite, act your best at all times, and help other kids act their best too. At the first hint of any talk about somebody hitting someone or a bunch of them ganging up on a kid, I keep the offending students in my room for a tough talk. The second time means isolation. I have the bullies sit at a designated table, facing the wall and without any interaction with the rest of the class. Third time, which is rare, I visit the home.

>> Tips

Turning bully bunches into beneficial bunches of students does not happen overnight, but many control bullies have traits of leadership, no matter how twisted. Straighten them out by asking them to lead in something positive, such as serving on an anti-bully committee to come up with ideas for the school to use.

BULLY Q AND A

Q: What makes a bully a controller?
A: The environment: that is, the home, school, and community.

Q: What stops a controller from being a controller?
A: The same things: the home, school, and community.

Unfortunately we can't do makeovers of all homes, although we can try, but we can definitely stop any controller's bully conduct at school and in the community.

Important: *Your students can help with identifying the toughest bully groups and their leaders in your school and community. Just ask them.*

ACTIVITY

Character Lessons

- Have a discussion in class, or with the class councils or student government, about the topic of conscience, that little voice inside us that tells us what's right and wrong. Discuss guilt, feeling ashamed, knowing what you did wasn't right, and then making it right. These types of discussions help in developing your students' character. Also, have students research the topic of conscience on Google.

- Ask the school counselor to visit the classroom for several weeks to teach empathy and listening skills to students. Use the model below as an example.

How to get CAUT as a good listener.

<u>C</u>aring

<u>A</u>ccepting

<u>U</u>nderstanding

<u>T</u>rust

- Discuss each of these traits and then pair up students and have them practice listening to each other.

- Ask students how they show these qualities while listening.

- Have all students learn these skills and then teach them to younger students.

Bully Type 3 – The Controller

>> Strategies

68 *Make sure all your kids are connected with at least one caring adult. Bullies who are controllers need to form relationships with adults they like and trust. Issue the first report card of the year to parents or guardians only. If no adult shows up for a particular student, find a neighbor, teacher, coach, or other concerned adult to show up and fill in for the missing adult.*

69 *Teach the bully leaders to control only themselves. Hand them note cards to keep with them, like cue cards to refer to, with their own written messages or with the following messages to prevent them from further group bullying:*
- *I don't want to let my coach down.*
- *I want to make my parents proud.*
- *I want to do the right thing, be smart, and be somebody.*
- *I want to help other kids.*

70 *Form an inter-club council with a representative from every school group, clique, club, and athletic team. This club's main agenda is to bully proof all extra-curricular activities which could be used to subtly or openly cause group bullying.*

Bully Type 3 – The Controller

>> Strategies

71 *Challenge the student body to go over the anti-bully rules in the student handbook with a fine-tooth comb and point out any loopholes in the rules for bullying, cyber-bullying and in the listed consequences. Are the bully leaders and bully groups addressed? What severe punishment is listed, and carried out, for a student making other kids participate in bullying?*

72 *Make bully prevention fun. Kids love to brainstorm and come up with all kinds of new ideas. They can plan a "Walk in My Shoes Day" or a "Beneath the Surface Day" when every student, teacher, staff member, and parent wears two different shoes or their jackets inside out, to show that we may all be different on the outside and yet we all share a huge commonality and importance.*

73 *Ask students to read stories written by authors from different locales and with different ethnicities to increase empathy and understanding. Begin by instructing your kids to ask people from all walks of life what their favorite book or author is/was. Post the results, then have kids add to that list.*

74 *Hold a "lunch 'n' meet"—a designated lunch time when kids sit at the cafeteria tables with students they usually don't associate with—twice a month. Also they can participate in a Mix It Up Day, where everyone sits with someone they don't know. The purpose is to break down toxic groups, clubs, and clique behaviors. Too many kids mingle only with their crowd and if it is powered by a bully, negative outcomes can ensue.*

Bully Type 3 – The Controller

>> Strategies

75 *Have students sit together at lunch, depending on their birthday month. All those born in January sit at one table, those born in February sit at another table, and so forth. Ask the student government to prepare a big card for all those involved and be sure the cafeteria provides a sheet cake for the monthly birthday bash.*

76 *Students can also sit by the color of the paper slips handed out as they enter the lunch room. Whatever color they pick determines their particular lunch partner for that day. If they mingle with different groups, even if just for 20 minutes now and then, they see their common bond and may develop a spirit of camaraderie that could lessen the likelihood of bullying.*

77 *Involve the faculty and staff, parents, business folks, and other community members in the lively lunch time group mix. Ask students to suggest representatives from the various businesses--such as banks, apparel stores, high tech businesses, for example—who can then be the featured guests. Bully groups that connect with business groups tend to focus more on their positive future and career than on putting their peers down.*

Bully Type 3 – The Controller

QUOTE: Anthony M., Youth Minister/Camp Counselor (for 18 years)

"These days, kids are into texting hateful messages via their cell phone, IM, or in a chat room. One kid always starts it and then it spreads like wildfire and gets worse and worse. But not around me. Uh-uh. Any youth I work with gets a lesson on leadership and relationship construction, not destruction. After I talk to the group, I work one-on-one with the control freak kid that started it all. We never move on to the year's activities unless everybody's on the same friendly page. Takes effort but man, what rewards."

- Another idea is to have every cafeteria table to reserve permanently two seats for adults. Then ask the police force to pop in anytime and interact with the students during break or lunch. Same goes for the elderly—anyone who is interested. This includes college kids, retired educators, clergy, coaches, guidance counselors, and school nurses. All of them can make great strides toward solving the bully group problem by just being there.

>> Strategies

78

Ask student leaders to contact the school communities in your state or around the nation where incidents of relational aggression are less common. Ask your students to interview—via email—their peers in other systems as to how they are solving the bully group problem in their schools. Invite them to come to your school through a visit or a virtual visit through teleconference.

Bully Type 3 – The Controller

>> Strategies

79 *Appoint a few students to write and illustrate a no-bully booklet for groups and heads of groups, and hand it out to groups of younger kids. Begin with the grade level at which groups or teams first manifest themselves. Include all youth groups, even the Scouts and Brownies.*

80 *Have your school newspaper run a series of teacher features that deals with eliminating bully leaders and gangs from school. To begin, send a survey to all faculty and ask them to respond to these questions: "Were you ever the target of a controlling bully or a bully group? If so, do you mind sharing this experience with the students?"*

- <u>Warning:</u> Any group bully act that goes unreported multiplies even worse than an individual bully act. It's like igniting a fire at various points at the same time and watching the flames coalesce.

81 *Counteract all bully group tendencies by getting as many students as possible involved in positive groups. Start a newcomers club, a planned kindness club, a true-school-spirit club, or similar groups. The more beneficial bunches there are, the less damage the mean cliques can do.*

82 *Have students design tee shirts or bumper stickers with an anti-bullying message. Initiate a contest with this theme and exhibit all entries in the school lobby. Ask community representatives to be the judges. Hand out cards or stickers with this message.*

Bully Type 3 – The Controller

>> Strategies

83 | *Start a club for bully proofers. One or two students in each class can be asked to volunteer for this club whose purpose is to learn the best bully preventing techniques and form an anti-bully corps. The kids can meet weekly and report on the latest relational aggression issues in their school and on the swift improvements made.*

84 | *Dedicate the first fifteen minutes of the first school day of each month to the topic of "No More Bullying." Use the worksheet on the next page to encourage your kids to stand up to bully behavior.*

QUOTE: Jim B., P.E. Teacher/Coach (for 21 years)

I tell my teams right off that any bullies or co-bullies will be cut, no questions asked. Then I hand out a sheet that lists what bullying is: teasing, taunting, threats, hazing, punching, shoving, mean texting, ugly Facebooking, anything at all that's disrespectful to another player, etc. Co-bullies are kids that witness bully conduct but don't tell. I want neither bullies nor co-bullies on any of my teams. Works like a charm.

Section 2: Four Types of Bullies

Worksheet

No More Bullying Worksheet

Pretend you're a controlling type of bully, either a top boy bully or a mean chick clique leader.

1. Whom do you control and how do you do it? _____

2. Why do you do this and what do you try to get out of it? _____

3. What should be your consequence? How could this consequence cause you problems? _____

4. What could you do next time to get the attention you want without hurting others? _____

Pretend you're the kid that is bullied by a group.

1. Who hurt you and how? _____

2. Why do you think they picked on you? _____

3. What do you think should happen to the bullies? _____

4. Whom can you tell about it to make it stop? _____

Pretend you're a spectator, watching a group of bullies turn on a kid.

1. What do you see going on? _____

2. What can you do besides watch? _____

3. What do you get out of watching? _____

4. What better things could you have done? _____

Pretend you're the bully ender, someone familiar with the bully do's and don'ts.

1. What did you observe? _____

2. What did you do to stop it? _____

3. What could you do to prevent the bully bunch's behavior long-range? _____

4. How do you feel knowing that something you did stopped the bully gang? _____

Bully Type 3 – The Controller

DISCUSSION QUESTIONS

1. Boys outnumber girls in athletic participation. Girls outnumber boys in other extracurricular activities, such as student government, the arts, academic clubs, yearbook/journalism, etc. Since in most schools athletics get the most publicity, many girls don't get the recognition they deserve. One example is the football pep rallies. Another example is the daily announcements in schools that highlight the latest sports victories but rarely the club achievements. What school-wide changes can be made to make girl groups feel more respected?

2. In addition to the bully problem in our schools, we have to address other areas which may be related. They include peer pressure, alcohol, drug addiction, early sexual activity, smoking, eating disorders, obsession with video games, violent movies, and the internet, poverty, gang recruiting, and weapons access. What should be done to solve these problems?

3. Many girls and boys, who are bullied repeatedly, especially by a group, feel helpless, hopeless, sink into depression, and consider hurting themselves and do. How can you find out who the most depressed students in your school are, what bully behavior directed at them is to blame, and how you can give them help and hope?

>> Tips

Too often students are reluctant to report a bully group because they want to be part of that group, even if it's a questionable bunch. Better to have some friends than no friends at all, is their reasoning. Discuss the characteristics of true friends and toxic friends. Start the conversation by using the worksheet on the next page.

Section 2: Four Types of Bullies

Stop the Mean Bunch Worksheet

Have you observed a group acting like bullies at school?_____

Do you belong to a group like that?_____

If yes, what makes you like this group?_____

_____

Would you like to belong to another group at school? Which one?_____

_____

What kind of new club or group would you like to see at your school? _____

_____

What can you do by yourself to stop a bunch of kids from bullying?_____

_____

What can you do—by working with others—to stop a mean bunch?_____

_____

How many more nice groups, than mean groups, are there in your school? Name them.

_____

Bully Type 3 – The Controller

>> Strategies

85 Make sure all your students are involved in at least one fun and meaningful extra-curricular activity that has a positive purpose. Compare the club- and team rosters to the school membership and see what the difference is. How many kids are left out? Meet with these kids and find out their interests, maybe form a new club.

86 Provide a place and time for the bully group leaders to shine. Call them together or counsel them individually. Teach them to concentrate on making personal progress and not on controlling their peers. Give them a personal success chart to follow and check in with them every so often, and acknowledge their successes.

87 Arrange for counseling for the victims of a controlling bully or crew. This can be individual counseling or in a group setting. Just like the leader of the bullies needs to be re-educated, the victims also need a special looking after. If you are pressed for time—and what educator isn't?—begin with the victims--always. They deserve your attention first. Teach victims how to be assertive and confident.

88 Go beyond bully proofing just the classrooms. The lunchroom, the hallways, the gym and the schoolyard are too often the real bully arenas. Check them out during their busiest times. Of course, many controlling bullies will put on a "nice act" when they see you. Therefore, show up often, or send someone to stand in for you. That "nice act" may actually become ingrained after a while.

Bully Type 3 – The Controller

>> Strategies

89 *Teach the whole school staff to watch out for any unusual behavior in kids. Design a rubric for teachers, parents, coaches, and others about what to look for in the conduct of our young that indicates they have been bullied. Have the guidance counselor network with other professionals to come up with a check list of red flags to look for.*

90 *Just like you recruit substitute teachers, recruit some substitute parents—moms and dads who are good parents and could do a world of good for any under-parented student. Explain to them that their talents are much needed and ask them if they're willing to take on the long-range overseeing of a child or two that seem seriously under-parented.*

91 *Educate yourself about the gang problem in your area. City after city and county after county across the country now feel the effects of an ever-widening gang presence that has its roots in our schools. What are the signs of gang activity in schools? Ask a gang expert to address this at your next faculty meeting.*

Bully Type 3 – The Controller

>> Strategies

92

Strengthen your rapport with the community by initiating programs such as:

- *"Coffee with the Principal and Teachers," a weekly breakfast, open to parents and other members of the community*
- *"Lunch & Learn," a get-together to reach out to the community and pull people in, where bully problems are discussed*
- *"Fun Field Days," bus trips away from school which include picnics and an array of wacky competitions that unite kids and community chaperones in laughter*
- *Longer school days/years but with different offerings that reflect the interests and true talents of the kids*

>> Tips

These days, many students come from single-parent homes, and many of those single moms and dads have two jobs just to make ends meet. Therefore, expand the PTA work and influence as much as possible by asking the members to invite athletes from colleges or other stars—exactly the kind of dynamos kids look up to—as guest speakers. Prepare your students for the speakers by using the worksheet on the next page.

Section 2: Four Types of Bullies

Role Models Worksheet

Whom do you admire most? Why? _____

_____

Who is next on your list of people you admire? Why? _____

_____

Would you like for younger kids to look up to you? Why? _____

_____

What makes a person a hero? _____

_____

_____

What heroes/heroines in history can you name? _____

_____

Have you ever done something special or observed someone else do something special?
Give details. _____

_____

_____

What figure in literature (or in movies or on TV) do you admire? _____

_____

What quality in yourself would you like to improve so that someday you may be in a
position to do something special for others? _____

_____

Bully Type 3 – The Controller

>> Strategies

93 *Call the civic groups and faith-based organizations in the area, ask to meet with them, and establish a solid connection. That way, you may be informed about any bullying going on outside school or any gang-related activities on the horizon. Many high schools in this country, and an increasing number of middle schools, report escalating gang problems that are frequently overlooked.*

- While the National Center for Education Statistics reports that 29 percent of students reported street gangs being present at their schools in 1995, the guesstimate in education circles now is 50 percent, especially in urban schools. But when the whole community is linked up to the school house, news of trouble brewing flies fast and can be dealt with—fast.

94 *Identify those adults in the community who have a knack for dealing with bully leaders. Have those adults coach the control-freak bullies on a weekly basis and direct them to school success. Tap into all the special inspirational powers that exist in your wider circle.*

>> Tips

One reformed bully leader or mean-chick clique leader can influence many other kids for the better. That same beneficial influence exists in grandparents. Match one or two of them up with bully leaders who have no adult connection. Also, encouraging striving young people to fill the void in the lives of younger under-parented kids helps. Many schools now require volunteering as part of graduation. So college kids can connect to high schoolers, high school seniors to freshmen, freshmen to middle schoolers, and so on down. Then no child will be left behind and none will be disconnected from society and feel like they have to gain attention by gathering a bunch of co-bullies around and brutally terrorizing smaller or less popular kids.

Bullying, no matter if it is verbal or physical, or carried out by a vicious group with a controlling leader, is a symptom of trouble. This symptom must be addressed. If it is swept under the rug over and over, the most pernicious type of bully may emerge and wreak havoc not only on one classroom, school, or state. He or she can deliver a stunning blow to our whole nation. Yes, the most egregious school bully can do unthinkable damage.

Bully Type 4 – The Potential Killer

Insight

The most dangerous bully in our schools is the potential killer. This type of kid is a rare case, but the potential to kill can exist in every educational setting. This particular troubled student may have started out dissing other kids without anyone paying attention. Next in the chain of events might have come hitting and lashing out physically against his/her peers, and again, nothing of consequence was done.

After that, the escalating bully may have allied him/herself with some followers at school. Or quite often, this type of bully can attract a circle of allies by surfing the net. These days, a student's bad friends don't have to be physically present. They can be chat-room bullies or bloggers who are avowed admirers of Columbine or other school killings.

But even then, no one intervened in the potential school killer's life until it was too late and he/she mowed down a classmate or more than one. In fact, far too many young lives have recently been lost needlessly, too many families have been left in ruins, too many people physically and psychologically scarred for the rest of their lives, and too many communities have had to cloak themselves in permanent mourning.

Indeed, the chain of victims of school killers stretches across our nation because no state is an island. But according to a column in the <u>Herald-Sun</u> in Durham, NC:

> **You can stop the next school shooting: One person. A teacher or a guidance counselor. Or a coach or a minister. A neighbor. Just one single human being. That's all it would have taken to prevent the [latest] school shooting. Just one man or one woman. Just one single person. Just one...**
>
> **Remember, one person can make a start.**

One person can try!

A student who bullies or is bullied can turn into a potential killer when the circumstances are just plain wrong. He/she can be a lonely potential killer or connect with, or control, other disturbed kids, but the outcome is tragically always the same.

Bully Type 4 – The Potential Killer

Bully Story

ENDLESS BULLYING

In August 2008, a 15-year old student shot and killed another 15-year old student as his classmates and friends stood around and watched, horrified. This tragedy happened shortly after 8 a.m. one morning in the cafeteria of Central High School in Knoxville, Tenn. The victim suffered from a condition that caused severe hair loss and had been the target of nonstop teasing since childhood.

Although many more details are available about this terrible incident, we sadly don't need more information. The few sentences above suffice to tell the story. It's most likely one of a kid being taunted mercilessly, of bullying going unchecked for years, and of extreme violence being the end result and of an unnecessary death having the last word.

But also most likely this whole scenario could have been prevented. The resulting needless suffering, pain, and death could have been avoided, and the innocent bystanders wouldn't have been traumatized for years, maybe even for life.

>> Tips

Even before the shockwaves surrounding this particular school shooting ebbed off, more incidents of kids bringing weapons to school were reported in the media. Certainly not all of the gun-packers were intent on shooting their classmates, but many of them were. So, knowing the red flags of any potentially violent student is crucial. Post this list, so you and other staff can see it.

The Pre-violence Warning Signs

- Being a bully or being bullied

- Sudden withdrawing from friends and peers

- Feeling very much alone: "Nobody understands me."

- Feeling rejected and excluded from cliques, clubs, and activities

- Continued poor school achievement/attendance

- Expressing violent thoughts in drawings, journal writings, stories, texting, or self-produced videos.

- Being addicted to violence in movies, on TV, and in video games

- Having mounting anger that keeps escalating

- Having many discipline problems that seem to worsen

- Being prejudiced

- Using drugs and alcohol

- Associating with gangs

- Easy access to weapons

- Making serious threats, either verbally, written, or text messaged.

Of course, not all of the above signs crop up in kids
that potentially go on to kill, but it pays to be aware of all of them.

Bully Type 4 – The Potential Killer

>> Strategies

95 Build a solid anti-bullying school and community foundation by implementing a tough consequences-for-the-bullies program. This approach needs to be of the escalating kind, with the consequences getting tougher as the severity of bullying increases. Then train all staff in the protocol. It often solves most of the problems associated with the dissers, the hitters, and the controllers.

96 For the toughest bullies, a very small percentage, who may have deep-rooted physical or other problems, intervene very early on—in 1st, 2nd, 3rd, 4th or 5th grade. Keep precise records of what methods have been tried to de-bully these kids and pass them on to administrators, teachers, guidance counselors, school nurses, psychologists, and school resource officers. Check up on what became of those kids every few months. Deeply ingrained bully problems are not outgrown, only out-worked, out-strategized, and out-singled. Underlying medical issues may need to be addressed as well and intense, long-term counseling may be needed.

97 Intervene immediately with the one scary bully in your school who has such huge emotional and conduct problems that, in spite of your very best efforts, he/she gets worse day by day. Have that walking time bomb removed from your school and placed into an educational setting able to deal with him/her. Of course, have all documents and observations in place.

Bully Type 4 – The Potential Killer

>> Strategies

98
Address the dropout problem that can affect as many as 40% of students in some school districts. Even in the early grades, pre-dropouts can be spotted. They often are either bullies or bullied, fall behind in their school skills, and can turn to violence.

>> Tips

Remember the "good old days"? Back then, minor bullies could be suspended temporarily which often cured them and major bullies could be kicked out of school permanently—another solution, at least for the victims.

But not any more: now there is no one at home to discipline them. Therefore, kicking kids out means they learn worse behavior on the "mean" streets, the street corners, and the malls—which all are the new staging areas for bullies, gangs, and young criminals.

The internet, which is accessible from home, the libraries, and internet cafes, can also be a place for the worst bullies, vandals, and gang members to exchange dreadful ideas. Much hate speech, racial slurs, and threats are first posted on the web.

BITING THE BULLIES
Dead-serious bullies do not stop wanting to either hurt innocent kids or those who have slighted them, unless they feel the bite of real consequences early on in their bully development. So swift and severe emergency measures must be in place. Therefore, use all resources and possible solutions in a planned approach and involve all connected parties—the parents, other relatives, mental health workers, educators, coaches, and law enforcement. You must find a solution to any super bully even if it means devoting yourself to that particular problem kid nonstop. This child may be just a tiny step away from taking a life.

Bully Type 4 – The Potential Killer

>> Strategies

99 *Find out what the overall violence potential is at your school. Is it high or low? Is it increasing or getting better? Survey your students anonymously and over time with the help of the worksheet on the next page.*

- Compile the results and share them with your staff. If the first eight questions are answered with a yes, a climate of pre-violence exists in the school environment of the responder. All Yes answers are minus-points and indicate problem areas.

- In contrast, a yes to question # 9 is a sign of hope.

100 *Many potential killer kids have no clear vision of the future. They see their life as ending shortly. So they live day by day, without ever looking ahead and expecting some joyful times or accomplishments in the days to come. Help your students to picture a good and long life ahead, one that is productive, by using the worksheet on page 86.*

QUOTE: Connie P., Principal (for 26 years)

 On the first day of school, I hold an assembly. I stress that every member of my school is a valuable citizen and anyone who bullies one of my students bullies me personally. That means they are in serious trouble. Next I hand out a list of strict consequences. That alone cuts the bullying down by more than two thirds. I also ask my staff to notify me immediately concerning any threats or potential physical harm or if there's any hint of a weapon brought on campus. ''

Risk Survey

	YES	NO
1. Could you get your hands on a gun if you wanted to?		
2. Are you picked on a lot?		
3. Do you take drugs or wouldn't mind taking them?		
4. Do you drink alcohol?		
5. Do you hate school?		
6. Do you spend a lot of time without a parent or other adult around?		
7. Do you think about committing suicide?		
8. Do you know of any gangs at your school or in your neighborhood?		
9. Is there an adult at school that you can talk to whenever something or someone is bothering you a lot?		

Section 2: Four Types of Bullies

Your Future Worksheet

What do you want to do this summer? (I don't know is not an acceptable answer.)

_____

What present do you want to get for your next birthday? Why? Be specific.

_____

What do you want to do when you turn 8, 10, 13, 16, 19, 21, 25?
(Choose three years and tell why.) _____

_____

_____

What type of work would you like to do now if you could? Why?

_____

What do you want to do after you finish high school?

_____

What would you like to study in college? Why?

_____

What kind of work would you like to do as an adult?

_____

Is it more important to make lots of money or do work you like? Why?

_____

In the future, if you could have two careers, what would they be?

_____

Bully Type 4 – The Potential Killer

>> Strategies

101 *Share some stories of children who accidentally killed a friend with a firearm. The Media Specialist may have some newspaper reports available. Enlist the PTA, other parents, teachers, and concerned adults in your effort to address the availability of guns for kids. Guns or other weapons lying around and a negative or revenge-seeking mentality can create a lethal mix. Have someone from the police department hold a workshop on gun safety. Include what students should do immediately if they see a gun or know a student who has a gun.*

>> Tips

Immediately make a note of all your kids who say they hate someone. "I hate happy people," is the way one potential killer bully described his very troubled outlook on others. What he probably meant was students who seemed content, had friends, and were productive. In other words, he abhorred exactly what he was not. He expressed in his journal how deep his dislike was, and that his feelings increased as to his "want/need to kill people." Too bad no one interceded. No one recognized the red flags. Before long, he allegedly ended up murdering almost all members of a family that he thought had what he didn't—happiness and normalcy.

WARNING SIGN:
When a student expresses his/her desire to kill someone or themselves—verbally or in a journal or blog, in a drawing or as part of a homework assignment—the threat must to be taken seriously. (Exception: Rare casual joking in a trivial context, such as in "If you don't give me a piece of bubblegum right now, I'll kill you.")

Bully Type 4 – The Potential Killer

>> Strategies

102 *Do whatever you can to make kids aware of the good things in their lives, by handing out the worksheet on the next page for them to fill in.*

>> Tips

Just having metal detectors at the entry of a school and preventing kids from bringing guns to school is not enough. Bullied kids can become so desperate that they go to extreme measures. They can smuggle razor blades or box cutters onto the school grounds by concealing them in hollowed-out books or paper bags to sneak in during Open House or other after-school events when security might be laxer.

Some kids try their hardest to find a gap in the security system at school. They survey the whole campus, discover an unsupervised back fence, and throw knives or other lethal weapons over it, then hide their arsenal in a gym bag.

103 *Check every week to make sure your school has not developed a hole in its safety plan. That requires frequent physical checks of all buildings and the whole campus. Mount a wall chart to post the inspection dates. Ask an assistant to do the same. Sometimes we don't see what's right before us and two sets of eyes see more than one.*

Section 2: Four Types of Bullies

Gratitude Worksheet

What is great about your life? _____

What is not so great? _____

Who or what makes it great or not so great? _____

_____

Whom are you grateful to and for what? _____

Write a paragraph thanking the person who is making your life great.

_____

_____

_____

_____

_____

_____

Who has been the biggest positive influence for you over the years? _____

Who outside your family and friends is a good influence to you? _____
Write this person a short note of appreciation.

Picture yourself someday being a role model to a young kid.
What would you want them to admire about you? _____

_____

_____

Be sure the thank-you and appreciative notes are mailed or forwarded to the appropriate people.

Bully Type 4 – The Potential Killer

>> Strategies

104

Involve the whole staff in a periodic security check-up by asking them to find the answers to these questions:
- *Do we have enough metal detectors?*
- *Are the video-cams in the building and on campus strategically placed and working?*
- *What is the background and experience of the resource officers and school guards?*
- *Is every member of the staff up-to-date on the latest security threats and red flags?*
- *What internet security programs are in place at school? At the homes of the students?*
- *How well informed is the whole student body about safety issues?*
- *Have faculty members question every 10th student and report their findings.*

>> Tips

The student body in any school is the most underused resource in the reporting of a bully with potential murder on their mind. Students also know better than anyone else on campus where the most dangerous bully spots might be. Just ask them.

105

Create an Advisor/Advisee program throughout the school where each teacher meets with a select group of students each morning or afternoon at a designated time. This provides a time for the teachers to get to know the students on a more personal level and to discuss personal concerns. Each year students should be able to select from a list who they want as an advisor the next year. This program allows students to connect with one caring adult in the school. Many times that is what the bully really wants, someone to listen.

Bully Type 4 – The Potential Killer

>> Strategies

106

Take some time in class to have students showcase their talent, hobby or something they can do well. Encourage all students to participate. Tell the students ahead of time that as long as what they share is appropriate it doesn't matter how strange or weird their interests may seem. You can learn so much about the student's world by doing this. It also allows students to connect and learn more about each other and can help break down barriers. Students are more likely to report a potentially harmful or dangerous situation if they feel more personally connected to that person.

107

Send home a copy of the survey on the next page to ten percent of the student body and enclose a stamped return envelope. Use the results to beef up your security measures.

108

Instruct your students to pretend they have seen another student, or an adult, with a weapon on campus. Tell them exactly what to do in this case, then test them to see if they can follow the prescribed steps. Do this exercise—as a rehearsal—every semester. Before this test, be sure to notify the parents in advance—no need to scare them.

>> Tips

In some school systems the administrators are so overworked that they feel like they have to leave certain parts of the school or campus unsupervised or neglected. As a result, skipping class, fist fighting, and weapon brandishing and all sorts of illegal activities seem to be condoned in these areas.

Studying a floor- and campus plan and securing every corner with a call box can help to reclaim each questionable education space.

Section 2: Four Types of Bullies

How Safe is Your School?

Is there any place in your school or building, or on the grounds, that doesn't feel safe?

_____

Why do you have that feeling? _____

_____

What do you do if you have to go near that spot? _____

_____

Are there enough cameras in the halls of your school, or are there no man's land corners?

_____

Are there enough metal detectors to make you feel safe? _____

*How often do you see a police officer or security guard patrolling the campus?*_____
The parking lots? After school, when you have practice for band, tennis, cross-country, etc.?

_____

Draw a map of your school and indicate where you think the unsafest spots are.
Where might somebody wishing to harm somebody hide or get in? _____

*Has your teacher told you what the rules are in case of a safety emergency?*_____

Are these rules posted in your classroom? _____

Are there call boxes in every classroom you go to and do they work? _____

What else could be done to make your school, your building, and the grounds safer?

_____

Section 2: Four Types of Bullies

ACTIVITY

Bullying Questionnaire
(for Teachers and Staff)

• What incidents of bullying, verbal harassment, or fighting have you observed?

_____

• When and where did they occur?

_____

• How did they affect you and your students?

_____

• Who or what do you think started the incidents?

_____

• What did you do?

_____

• Why did you do this?

_____

• What do you think can be done to prevent further incidents of bullying or fighting?

_____

• Do you feel prepared to deal with these kinds of incidents?

_____

• Would you like to take a course in bully prevention?

_____

Bully Type 4 – The Potential Killer

>> Strategies

109 *Enlist students and parents in beautifying the most neglected corners of your school with plants, new equipment, and fresh paint. Draw up a grid of the grounds and have clubs select a forgotten area to work on and to adorn. Assign some of your bully students as well. Many have talents and abilities that no one has tapped into.*

110 *Teach your students not only the bully red flags but also the warning signs for related problems, such as:*
- *depression*
- *eating disorders*
- *anxiety and stress*
- *self-injury*
- *suicide*

- The idea is **never** for kids to become the watchdogs of others and spy on them, but for all kids to support one another, so all of them can reach their true potential.

>> Tips

Bullying does tremendous damage. Some people report that being bullied in their youth reduced their focus on success in school by 30% or more, but let's assume it was only 20%. Multiplied by the roughly seven percent of the US population who admits to being bullied and rounding down the population to 300 million, that is 21 million people whose scholastic success was diminished by 20 %. What a staggering amount of lessened or lost potential that is, and we haven't even begun to add up all the damage done to the spectators.

Just think of all the difficult issues in science, medicine, economics, and US energy production, for example, that cry out for a solution.

Bully Type 4 – The Potential Killer

QUOTE: Brandon R., School Resource officer (for 21 years)

Kids killing kids can often start over nothing. I've got a file of cases where minor dissing escalated to a major fuss. Then guns come into play, you know. So I preach the importance of no trash talking. When I talk to kids, I use real examples of when the lack of respect caused a mighty bad ending. Prevention is key—always. No telling how many young people wouldn't be in jail or the emergency room or the cemetery right now, if they'd been taught to get a grip on their lips.

DISCUSSION QUESTIONS

1. In too many homes sibling bullying goes on which can affect girls more than boys because frequently brothers are physically stronger than their sisters. How can we stop sibling bullying?

2. There is also boyfriend or girlfriend bullying. Too many girls, and some boys, accept the controlling or threatening behavior of their dates without ever saying a word. They hide their bruises with long sleeves, and their black eyes with make-up. What can be done to change that?

3. Untreated bullies often grow up into adult bullies and take their relational aggression into the world of work. As a result, many work places are poisoned by male and female office bullies. What can be done to discourage adult-to-adult bullying, violent behavior directed at women, workplace brawls and potential job-related shootings?

Section 3: Conclusion

Your bully proof work is on the road to success when all three segments of the process have been addressed. They are:

1. Bully awareness and knowledge of the four types of bullies and their modus operandi

2. Bully intervention, including solid reporting methods and clear, strict consequences that are carried out by everyone

3. Bully prevention, that means initiatives that preclude bully acceptance and a school vulture culture, through early action at the elementary level

>> Strategies

Do Sweat the Bullies

111 *So that the no-bully theme permeates the whole school campus, hand out book marks with a bully-free logo, along with the textbooks. Have students design and submit samples of book marks. Ask teachers and other staff to participate too.*

112 *Honor each classroom that goes a month without having a single student reported for bullying by placing a bully proofed decal (with the month and year displayed) on the door. Take a photo of that classroom door and display it in the office with the caption: Well Done! This Room Sent Bullies on the Run!*

>> Strategies

113

Announce any bully-free progress that is reported over the intercom by giving a statistical analysis. For example, announce this: Last year at this time, we had 20 bully reports. This year, only ten so far. That is a reduction of 50%. The biggest improvement was on the ___ grade level (fill in). Therefore all ___ graders (fill in) will have an extra morning break of 15 minutes today.

114

Make plans for the bully backsliders, which are to be expected, and praise all kids who help others to refrain from bullying and backsliding. Usually former bullies will revert to bullying now and then. Be prepared by having an action plan outlined for them—beforehand. Maybe these students can share with younger students how they became a bully.

115

Once a month, print a flyer about all hallways or buildings that have gone for four weeks without a single bully incident. Declare those areas bully proofed and hang up bully-free banners. Move these banners to the auditorium to highlight them at the assemblies.

116

Ask the student council to design wristbands to be awarded to all groups, sports teams, clubs, and cliques that have eliminated bullying from their ranks--totally. Have a special Wristband Day, when clubs and other groups with a bully-free climate get recognized.

>> Strategies

117 *Every so often, test your students' bully awareness by asking them to name the different kinds of bullying. (For example: girl bullying, sexual bullying, racist bullying, homophobic bullying, technological bullying, subtle bullying, in-your-face bullying, hazing, harassing, girl friend- and boyfriend bullying, and so on) Give extra credit for students who bring in newspaper articles or other literature.*

118 *Ask the art club to create paper flowers to present to people in their neighborhood who are especially nice, and to store personnel that goes out of their way to be considerate. The remedy for bullying is extending kindness and appreciation to as many people as possible.*

119 *Have post cards printed to mail home to parents whose kids are giving up their bully ways and are now starting to show good leadership. Don't mention the bullying problem on the post cards—only the improved leadership qualities. E-mail messages will work as well. You've got mail, of the positive type.*

QUOTE: Manuela R., Teacher Assistant (for 9 years)

" I'm so grateful to anyone who works in bully prevention. Everyone needs to understand that bullying is a horrible reality in our schools. Kids everywhere suffer from it daily. So many parents don't realize their child could be a school bully. They need to get involved—now. "

Section 3: Conclusion

>> Strategies

120 *Have a presentation on __Bullycide__, all students who commited suicide because of being bullied. Invite a speaker from __Bullycide in America__ to come to your school to talk to students about the seriousness of bullying. (www.bullycideinAmerica.com)*

121 *Facebook and cyber bully-proof your school by each day publicizing a reminder or hot tip for students and teachers to use. A parent volunteer can read the reminder/tip over the intercom to reinforce the idea that in bully-proofing the whole school community acts as one. And Facebook entries should be acceptable and not be painful arrows, intended to hurt.*

>> Tips

While many schools claim they are too busy or too poor to bully proof, they need to realize that their school scores will soar once they are bully proofed. Getting rid of the vulture culture frees kids to concentrate on academic success. Plus, discipline problems will decrease. Your whole school will be welcoming and nurturing, not worrisome and nasty.

Bully proofing your school will raise its satisfaction scores as well. And how inspiring to see a big sign at a school entrance: "The Bullying Stops Here" or "This Is a Bully Free Zone," or a line painted across the walkway leading to the school with this message: "No Bullying Beyond This Point."

What a source of pride for your students to realize that they helped to end the bullying. Using their power to stop peer-to-peer bullying ups their self-esteem. If they are allowed to design textiquette booklets that spell out the no-nos in texting, messaging, IMing, blogging, Face-booking, and picture posting, they will be even more enthusiastic.

It is important to have the bully girls and bully boys contribute to the booklets. If they are asked to explain the latest lingo, the fun-making language, and double meanings, they're being empowered to turn from bully-razzi—kid paparazzi armed with smoking cell phones—to high achievers. Who's got time to bully other kids when you're busy being your own personal best?

While you bully proof your school, take time to address other school issues. Examine the student ID's and staff ID's. Are they copy-proof? Are visitors' ID-tags collected at the end of the day? Are the visitors' reasons for being at school verified?

In too many cases, complete strangers march into a school with no more than knowledge of a student's name—information they've gathered from Facebook—which they use as an excuse, saying they're dropping off lunch money. They sign in on the clipboard the harried office staff points to, without anyone probing into their background. Once they have received a pass, they're free to roam the hallways. But what if they're bent on violence?

The student and faculty parking lots need a close eye too. Are there spot-checks of student and staff vehicles, which could be used as weapons transport? Another issue is corporal punishment which is still permitted in many states. The question is, do kids learn from these old punishments or do they learn to bully?

The idea should never be student punishment but student advocacy and advancement. If bullying is looked at as a syndrome of something being wrong in the school environment, then solutions can be found.

Section 3: Conclusion

DISCUSSION QUESTIONS

1. Bully proofing has three parts: bully awareness, bully intervention, and bully prevention. What are weakest parts in your school? What are the strongest?

2. The same electronic gadgets kids use to bully can be used in bully eliminating. Can't reminders of the no-bully rules and consequences be emailed or text-messaged to students? How can your school's website incorporate a quick bully reporting link?

3. How do you celebrate all the bully improvements within your school, your school system, and the whole community?

>> Tips

Listening to the bullies is important. Their experiences matter. Maybe bullying is all they have ever observed. But just as a smoke-free environment can be created, so can a bully-free one. Students can learn new ways of behavior, and the younger they are, the faster the process. And what great benefits arise from a bully-free environment. When kids don't have to worry about getting teased, taunted, or terrorized, they can concentrate on their studies.

Therefore, after-school programs can't be just for kids not doing homework, or being tardy, or failing a class any more, but also for the bullies. Plus, a summer school program or a Saturday morning program for hardened bullies can be started. Only if the bullies really feel the negative consequences of being bullies will they think twice before they diss, hit, control others, or brandish a gun at school.

These days, schools are such hectic places with so much going on, and people, such as you, are often overworked and underpaid. What can you do as you gear up to bully proof your school? Copy the warning signs on the next two pages and post them, over and over.

1. LACK OF ADULT ATTENTION

Every child needs attention from at least one adult. That can be a mom or dad, grandparent, neighbor, guidance counselor, teacher, coach, or faith-based worker, or a substitute parent. But if the adult attention is only sporadic, lacking, demeaning, or punitive, the child will find other sources of attention, for example, attention from peers or a gang lurking as he/she walks home from school.

2. EMOTIONAL UNHEALTH

Approximately 20% of kids experience feelings of depression, especially during their teens, according to the website www.teendepression.org. Of course, almost all kids have feelings of sadness now and then. It's when those feelings lead to depression that lasts for more than two or three weeks, that it's time to worry. Emotional unhealth that goes neglected can spur children on to negative behaviors. Parents and teachers need to keep a close eye on their kids and note on a calendar if their son, daughter or student seems depressed for more than a few days, especially if there is no reason like a failed test, a break-up with a best friend, or the death of a pet.

3. EASY ACCESS TO WEAPONS

Easy weapons' access is a big factor in the bullying and violence potential in our children. So it has to be considered. Even if your children have been taught never to touch a gun unless you're there, what can you do about their friends or the children of the yard crew or the neighbor?

Besides, guns are only a small problem. Bomb making directions and lists of common, yet dangerous chemicals are on line, so don't let your kids have unlimited entry to perilous sites.

4. ALIENATION AT SCHOOL

This warning sign shows itself in low grades and poor attendance. Parents should study their child's report card carefully. Just signing a bad report card, or allowing children to forge mom's or dad's signature, is tantamount to not taking a child with a broken leg to the hospital, or worse. Low grades and attendance are such clear red flags that schools also need to jump into action and intervene with any student who show signs of failure or truancy.

The school attendance officer who visited the homes of the school skippers is mostly gone. So are homeroom periods when teachers could guide students to achieve school success. Now every extra minute is used for instruction, and this at a time when fewer parents parent like they used to. Additionally, there is a huge reduction in guidance time. In the past, guidance counselors could spend hours counseling turned-off students. But with the increased testing mandates too many counselors report that over one third of their time is taken up by state test administration and the rest by student emergencies, most of which are due to bullies. That means kids starting to fail or skip class can be overlooked or left behind to fall between the cracks.

When school is so user-unfriendly that kids can ditch class or fail and nothing is done about it, immediate action is called for. How simple to have a list of underachieving and under-attending students printed out. Then solutions can be implemented.

5. NEGATIVE INFLUENCES

From 2nd and 3rd grade on, kids turn to their friends more and more. In the past, that development occurred later. Now it starts extra early because many kids mature faster. One reason is that in former times, adult information was delivered mainly through newspapers, magazines and in the form of books—all too difficult for small children to read. Back then, childhood was a time of protection.

Now from the time they're born, children are "adultisized"—overwhelmed with nonstop news and all its blood and gore. By the time they are seven, they have seen more horrendous tragedies on TV than their parents and grandparents did during their lifetime. Plus, the Internet offers images far beyond what's age-appropriate to even the most mature kids. So, it is important to monitor your child's friends. They may have been exposed to many more lurid images than your child and can have a negative influence. So make sure your child's friends are not a bad bunch.

6. DESTRUCTIVE DOWNTIME

Many kids don't have enough free time. Make sure yours do. Free time can be creative-think time and relaxing, but what you don't want to happen is for kids to pick up violent pursuits. Examine what your kids do all day. Have them fill out a time sheet, on which they list what they do, half hour by half hour, for a week.

The latest research proves that kids who play violent video-games a lot tend to get into fights with other kids more often, or get into more trouble at school. While we cannot make a direct connection between bullies who watch killer video games and kids who kill, we need more positive activities for all of them. There are many hobbies and sports kids can get involved in, and so many fun brain-game activities for them to pursue. Insist that they do.

7. POOR ROLE MODELS

Sadly many students have no positive role models. Worse is, that in their absence, they will find their own. But if we don't guide them toward people with a positive influence, kids may choose to admire someone who has qualities you don't want your son/daughter or student to emulate.

Some children go so far as to idolize a historical figure that killed millions or a recent school shooter. Any teen idol vacuum can be filled with good images, as well as evil ones. Therefore, the more inspiring personalities your kids can meet, hear about, read or research about, the better. Exposing kids to top role models is key. When they have plenty of good role models, their inclination to bully and resort to violence plummets.

8. FUTURE LIMBO

Too many kids feel they have no future. They live moment by moment, barely hanging on, because nobody has ever taught them to focus on the years ahead. And that absence of plans for their future has a detrimental effect. But if every young person had a clear vision of a positive future, much bully potential and violence proneness could be eliminated. Why even think of ruining your shiny life ahead?

We must ensure that all kids have a plan for their future by talking to them about their potential, encouraging them to hone it, set clear goals and achieve success.

>> Tips

These warning signs are not only red flags for potential bullying and violence, they are also great opportunities to help our students. And these opportunities arise again and again, for bully and violence proofing is not a one-time job. But the harder you work at it, the more you learn to bully proof and insure the safety of your school and community.

Please post the warning signs in the lounge at work, or on the stall door in the toilet. Bully proofing is like an immunization program. It can prevent diseases, but we can't rest. New ways to bully and changes in society crop up constantly. For example, in the late 80's, girls said for the first time that they wanted to become professional football players, so an increased blurring of gender roles can now be observed. That leads to new questions, such as:

- *Are girls really as violent as boys?*
- *Are the causes of their violence different from those of boys or the same?*
- *Are the types of violence that girls exhibit different from those of boys or the same?*
- *Should the prevention tactics be different for female students, or the same?*
- *In the future, will girls surpass boys in the frequency and level of violent bullying and other bad behavior?*

Bully- and pre-violence proofing can be a blessing in disguise because the process demands that teachers, administrators, and parents take a closer look at all school issues, and not just those posed by their kids but also those by outside students and adults. We have to ask, for example, how bully proof is the bus system? The bus stop? The walk home?

The school food chain also needs checking. Are the delivery trucks examined before they enter the school grounds? Could the food storage facilities be breached and something toxic be added to school lunches? What about the water fountains—are they safe?

Could parents be bus or lunchroom monitors? Could they monitor after-school events, athletic events, or evening SAT prep classes?

WORST SCENARIOS/BEST SOLUTIONS

School leaders need to be pro-active. That means they need to review what to do in the worst scenario, for example, in the case of a:

- Natural disaster
- Terrorist attack
- Conventional threats such as a bomb threats or a bully armed and roaming the halls
- Chemical attack from disgruntled science students or an outsider sneaking in with Ricin or some other deadly chemical
- Biological or nuclear crisis, be it small-scale or of huge proportions

These days, each school has to have a powerful anti-bully program, a safe campus, evacuation plans, and other steps in place to insure student safety. As we close the bully holes, we can close the other cracks that unsafe conditions produce.

The good news is that each time a potential peril to our kids—be it in the form of bullies, unsafe conditions, a pre-violent culture, health concerns, or other threats—is dealt with, the academic achievement levels of our students soar more. Kids feel safe, respected, cared for, confident, and proud if their deep concerns are addressed.

Using the bully proofing process as a stepping stone can lead to fixing what else prevents the healthy development of our youngsters, such as the prevalence of drugs and drinking, the gang influence, the state of student and faculty dress (is a dress code needed?), smoking, and student conduct at dances. Also it's time to rein in our kids' language. Verbal bullying isn't only threats. It's also kids' using profanity. The space within our earshot is being defiled by ugly words, so our ears and minds are being bullied! Kids should substitute OK words, such as "rats, drat, my stars, man-oh-man," for not-OK words. Profanity should not be tolerated.

TOP STRATEGY: DESIGNATE AN NBA, NO-BULLY ADVOCATE

In every school there is at least one teacher, staffer, or PTA member who has a gift or a special interest in bully prevention. Identify that person. Is it you? Locate some funds to pay this no-bullying advocate (NBA) extra, just like coaches and yearbook/newspaper advisors are paid extra.

Relieve the NBA of other duties—maybe a class or two—so he/she has time to focus on bully prevention. Have the NBA gather copies of all successful bully-prevention programs from around the country. Send the NBA to national conferences that address boy and girl bullying. The NBA will then share the latest bully proofing tips and strategies with the faculty, the rest of the staff, the parents and the community, invite everyone in the community to get involved, and start a top program designed to stop bullying in its tracks.

<u>QUOTE:</u> Robert F. Kennedy

Every time we turn our heads the other way when we see the law flouted, when we tolerate what we know to be wrong, when we close our eyes and ears to the corrupt because we are too busy or too frightened, when we fail to speak up and speak out, we strike a blow against freedom and decency and justice.

**IF WE DON'T END THE BULLYING NOW,
OUR SCHOOLS WILL SELF-DESTRUCT.**

<u>QUOTE:</u> Mahatma Gandhi

Be the change you want to see in the world.

**IN THE CASE OF BULLYING,
"BRING ABOUT THE CHANGE YOU WANT TO SEE IN THE WORLD!"**

THIS IS THE TIME WHEN BULLYING ENDS.

My Mission, Continued: A Victim of War

SO WHAT HAPPENED TO THE CITY OF MY BIRTH?

Dating back to the year 805, Magdeburg was a prosperous city of 360,000 at the beginning of WWII. Situated 80 miles south of Berlin on the Elbe River, it was a railway and industrial center, proud of its metal works, sugar refining plants and zinc smelters, and the capital of Saxony in Prussia. It manufactured much of Germany's paper, textiles, synthetic oils, chemicals, glass, automobiles, cranes, elevators and armory.

Of course it was attacked frequently during WWII, but the warning system was excellent. Whenever the sirens blared, the people raced to their bunkers and cellars, and emerged when the all-clear signal was given. There were many losses of buildings and lives, but Magdeburg survived fairly intact until four months before WWII ended.

From the fall of 1944 on, it was obvious Germany was losing the war. Hitler's Third Reich lay in ruins. Yet on the evening of Jan. 16, 1945, a huge contingent of Royal Air Force (RAF) planes left England and headed toward eastern Germany. By that time, every German city with a population of more than 100,000 had been given a code name, the name of a fish. Magdeburg was "Young Salmon." It was the RAF's goal that evening.

At the same time, several squadrons of American bombers headed out from France to the same target. Whether the double attack was planned or coincidental is not known.

First the incoming planes destroyed all warning capabilities. Many people were already in bed when the attack came. By the time the first siren roared, the signal bombs—called "Christmas trees"—had already lit up every street bright as a sunny noon.

As the startled people scrambled for shelter, the city was attacked non-stop for 38 minutes— probably the most deadly 38 minutes in WWII. Fire bombs were dropped carpet-fashion. Section after section of the city ignited. One fireball could be seen 50 miles away. It created such winds that hundreds of people were sucked out of their houses and burned to death. Those who managed to flee to the bunkers and cellars were overcome by poisonous fumes. Whenever panicky mothers pushed their children through whatever opening they could claw into the fiery walls of their hide-outs and told them to run, the children came screaming back because the pavement on the streets had melted. So they all suffocated together.

All night long and most of the following week, the fire in Magdeburg raged on. Since the water mains had burst, nothing could be done to stop it. When the fire finally went out, the charred remains of 16,000 people were collected in buckets. Another 12,000 were wounded and thousands more were never accounted for. The population of 360,000 was reduced to 90,000 by the end of WWII. Only Cologne and Dresden, among German cities, suffered more destruction than Magdeburg.

What followed was an uninterrupted series of burials. After a few days, the city leaders gave up and concentrated on feeding the survivors. They dug a pit, dumped all the leftover bones in, and raked dirt on top.

I almost burned to death in that gigantic hell-on-earth fire. But my mother, like a salmon knows its time to swim upstream, sensed death in the air in early January 1945. So she grabbed her brood and got us out of harm's way just in time. A few months later she died. She was almost 42. I was six and found her dead in bed. I didn't know she had died, and tried to wake her up, hour after hour. To no avail.

Later I had to accept her death but I never accepted the horrible end result and injustice of mass violence or of individual violence. I never accepted it during my long teaching career when I was too busy to do something about it. And I don't accept it now when I have time to speak out. That's what propels me to fight young bullies. If they grow up unchecked, horrible violence may ensue. But if we bully proof our schools, we can, to a great degree, violence proof our society, our world. Thank you again for doing this crucial work!

To read more about Erika's experience read her memoir,
A German Tale: A Girl Surviving Hitler's Legacy.

In Memoriam

Eve Carson was a gifted and vivacious student leader and student body president at UNC-Chapel Hill, NC, who was killed tragically in 2008 by two high school dropouts who had been in serious trouble before, but fell through the cracks. Eve loved to dance. This is in her memory:

Eve's Dance

What do you do when you feel down?
Just picture Eve dancing and lose your frown

Eve did great things before she was killed
She was filled with such life and joy
Can't you feel it?

Now she dances to the voice of a child
The roar of students at a game gone wild
Can't you see her?

Live life to the fullest, be kind to people
Just do your best, that's Eve's request
Can't you hear her?

Whenever you feel down, just picture Eve
Watch her dancing with the rustling leaves
The moving clouds. And make her proud.

by Erika Karnes

References

Beane, Allan L. (2005). <u>The Bully Free Classroom</u>. Minneapolis, MN: Free Spirit Publishing Inc.

Cooper, Barbara, and Widdows, Nancy (2008). <u>The Social Success Workbook for Teens</u>. Oakland,CA: Instant Help Book

Karres, Erika V. Shearin (2005). <u>Fab Friends and Best Buds</u>. Avon, MA: Adams Media.

Karres, Erika V. Shearin (2004). <u>Mean Chicks, Cliques, and Dirty Tricks</u>. Avon, MA: Adams Media.

Karres, Erika V. Shearin (2000). <u>Violence Proof Your Kids Now</u>. Berkeley, CA: Conari Press.

Postman, Neil (1994). <u>The Disappearance of Childhood</u>. New York, NY: Delacorte, Vintage.

Randall, Kaye, and Bowen, Allyson A. (2007). <u>Mean Girls: 101½ Creative Strategies and Activities for Working with Relational Aggression</u>. Chapin, SC: YouthLight, Inc.

Senn, Diane. (2007) <u>Bullying in the Girl's World</u>. Chapin, SC: YouthLight, Inc.

Slocumb, Paul D. (2004) <u>Hear Our cry: Boys in Crisis</u>. Highlands, TX: aha! Process, Inc.

Taylor, Julia V. (2007). <u>Salvaging Sisterhood</u>. Chapin, SC: YouthLight, Inc.

About The Author

Erika Karres, Ed.D. is an award-winning educator, speaker and author with a heart-wrenching personal story. She taught in the public schools and on the college level for 35 years. She won numerous "Teacher of Excellence" awards and was honored by the Governor of North Carolina and the Governor of Kentucky. After the Berlin Wall came down, she was asked to teach in the formerly communist East Germany.

Dr. Karres received a BA in Education, M.Ed. and Ed.D. from the University of North Carolina at Chapel Hill, NC. She is a featured keynote speaker for the 3rd Annual National Conference on Girl Bullying & Other Forms of Relational Aggression in Las Vegas. She contributes to the Durham Rescue Mission, a place for the homeless, hopeless, and helpless in Durham, NC.

She has written across the spectrum—from advice columns to education manuals and parenting books. Her most popular book is Mean Chicks, Cliques & Dirty Tricks (available in Russian). Her other books include:

- *A German Tale: A Girl Surviving Hitler's Legacy*

- *Make Your Kids Smarter*
  (available in Spanish as Hijos Brillantes, and in Chinese)

- *Crushes, Flirts, and Friends: A Real Girl's Guide to Boy Smarts*

- *Fab Friends and Best Buds*

- *Everything Parent's Guide to Raising Girls: A Complete Handbook*

- *Violence Proof Your Kids Now*
  (available in Japanese)

- *A+ Teachers*

- *Memoir Star with Susan Bowman*
  (Working Manuscript)